KHALID HOSSEINI'S THE KITE RUNNER

A TESTIMONIAL TO TRAUMA

MANPREET SHARMA & NITHAN KUMAR

ISBN 979-888546970-8

to all those who suffered the turmoil of trauma...

Contents

Preface

The narratives of Khaled Hosseini especially his debut novel, *The Kite Runner* reflects the traumatising situation and oppression of people of Afghanistan due to the war over three decades with the Soviet invasion in 1989 and thereafter the series of civil wars. Khaled Hosseini was an Afghan-American novelist who represent the devastating conditions of Afghanistan in his writings, and who is able to give words to the traumatic situation of the people of his homeland. His novel *The Kite Runner* depicts not only the physical damages but also detailed the psychological damages, in the form of sexual abuse, mental torture, mass murder and child abuse due to the war in Afghanistan. Moreover, academic research and literary production about the effects of trauma presented in Afghan narratives is fairly limited in comparison to that of World Wars, Vietnam War and the Holocaust Studies. This thesis explores the textual representation of trauma both at individual and collective level and trauma as a site for constructing history in the novel *The Kite Runner.* The study has been conducted in the framework of trauma literary theory to analyze the select Afghan fiction in English. Following Cathy Caruth and Dominic LaCpra, according to whom literature serves as a site for belated enactment and witnessing of what can be referred to as unclaimed moment of trauma, the study analyzes the characters in the novel, to see how the trauma-hit characters narrates the ravages of war in Afghanistan, if these flashbacks and haunting of the past are in accordance with the trauma theory. As Caruth uses the image of the wound that cries out and addresses us in an attempt to tell us of a reality or truth that is not otherwise available, to indicate that trauma can only be understood through literary are symbolic language. The study investigates in detailed the characters in the novel, to show that Afghan fiction in English works against the collective amnesia by representing traumatic experiences and their impact on individual and communities in the war ravaged Afghanistan, thus dealing with and bringing forth the traumatic history that many people believe to be a matter of long forgotten past. The study also investigates the characters experience of trauma and portrayed by the novelist, its effects and the process of working out and acting through situation. To start this qualitative study outlines the major trauma related works of Caruth, LaCapra, Felman, Tal and Whitehead and then keeping in view the tenets of trauma theory, it goes on to trace the accounts of characters in the selected novel to study their reaction to the trauma of War in the light of coping with trauma mechanisms by Erikson as well as LaCapra theory of *Working Through*, to see how their flashbacks presents the records of history which can be verified through factual records also. The study concludes that trauma fiction unlike historical accounts serves as an alternative source to understand the history of a particular nation and traumatic narratives are incorporated with the undiluted records which are the rich source of information unlike presented in official accounts of history.

Acknowledgements

It is a genuine pleasure to express our deep sense of thanks and gratitude to several scholars, critics, writers and the members of our families. Besides, there are many others who have made this work successful. Special thanks are due to the publishers Notion Press, libraries and the faculty from Depatment of English, University of Jammu and HNB University Garhwal. Finally, but most of all, our thanks to Khaled Hosseini, author of the book on which our work is based.

CHAPTER ONE

INTRODUCTION

Unlike official account of history, fiction portraying War trauma serves as an alternative source for understanding both physical and psychological damages of War. Since the writers of War fiction puts a kaleidoscopic view in the psyche of traumatized characters, an analysis of these literary masterpieces no more remains a straightforward task. In order to analyze the select novel of Afghan-American novelist Khalid Hosseini in English, it is well in place to carry out this whole investigation in the framework of trauma theory and its related models. Therefore, it is apt to study trauma which is defined as not just a wound to the mind but a source of first hand records of details of traumatic incident.

A detailed analysis of research databases shows that most of the research on trauma fiction has been carried out in cases where the fictional narratives are related to the technological advance countries/Nations. A fare example of this is the research done during the 1990s such as Holocaust, World Wars, Vietnam and 9/11 issues.

This indifference towards the trauma of a less developed but equally war ravaged country like Afghanistan is against the spirit of trauma studies which according to caruth's

Unclaimed Experience Trauma Narrative and History published in (1995) "is neither an advocacy movement nor it is specific to a certain group of people as she says that we are implicated in each Others trauma" (caruth 24). Thus the driving force behind carring out this study has been to remain ethical to the spirit of trauma studies and cater for the trauma, as depicted in the select novel of a less developed but equally war ravaged country, Afghanistan. By analyzing the fictional portrayal of war-hit Afghan people, through their acting out and working through reaction towards trauma, augment history, it has been proposed that fictional representation of traumatized people work as a testimonial record that tell the untold history which can be verified through factual records.

Background to the study

Termed by many as the, "Graveyard of Empires the history and narrative of Afghanistan have been shrouded in 35 year long continuous war" (Imran and Xiaochuan 66). Afghanistan is known for its multi-ethnicity where different ethnic groups resided which according to Imran and Xiachuan, who asserted in their article entitled *"Analytic History of Origins of the Darkness in Afghanistan"* published in (2015) comprises of "Aimaqs (10%), Hazaras (10%), Uzbeks (10%), Tajiks (25%) and Pasthuns (40-45%) is known to historian and critics due to its invincible nature in front of all foreign forces which invaded Afghanistan" (Imran and Xiaochuan 66).

Nancy Hatch Dupree one of the pioneer historians of the history of Science and Technology in his book titled *"An Historical Guide to Afghanistan: Air Authority, Afghan Tourist Organization"* published in (1977) asserts that "Since mid 1700s the country has existed in the present form in south-central Asia when Ahmed Shah Durrani united the tribal factions of the country" (Dupree 98). Since then, the country's history is marked by prolonged wars. This has caused millions of Afghan civilians to leave their country for safe abodes in the adjoining countries and beyond.

According to Martin Ewan, one of the former officer of the British Diplomatic server, who served in Afghanistan in his most influential work " Afghanistan: A Short History of its People and Politics" published in (2002) asserts that, "Afghanistan has over its long history been a highway of conquest between, west central and southern Asia" (Ewan 10). This has led to the dismal condition of the people of Afghanistan, who even today, are going through the trauma of similar war. Farhoumand in his research work titled *"Unfulfilled Promises Women and Peace in Post-Taliban Afghanistan"* published in (2005) asserts that, "the Soviet occupation of Afghanistan undermines the living standard of the people residing in the country, adding that human rights violations have been worst at the civil war that followed the occupation" (Farhoumand 62). Even after the withdrawal of Soviet forces from Afghanistan in 1889, the country fell into the prey to internal conflicts, which to prolonging the problems of the people in Afghanistan. Such a long exposure of the ravages of war has been collectively been recorded in history, but it is the fiction arising from this land that provides the true accounts of psychological trauma of the people of Afghanistan due to war.

Detailed inquiries into the devastation caused by these wars in the form of comprehensive historical research, highlighting the ravages of war during 10 years long Soviet occupation of Afghanistan and the consequent civil wars, have been carried out by the Afghan Civil Society Forum (ACSF), The Afghan Peace and Democratic Act (APDA),

The Association for the Defence of Women's Rights (ADWR), The Corporation Centre for Afghanistan (CCA), The Education Training Centre for Poor Women (ECW). This report covers a range of problems which the people of Afghanistan faced due the war from (1979-2009). The collective efforts made by these organization was pen down by Ashley Jackson of Oxfam International and the report was published under the title *"The Cost of War: Afghan Experiences of Conflicts"*(1978-2009) where in it the report highlights/outlines the destruction caused by 10 years long war in the following words:

After decades of relative stability, and the overthrow of Dauod Khan in 1778 and the subsequent invasion by Soviet forces in 1979 marked the beginning of a prolonged period of conflict, as mujahedeen resistance groups grew in strength, waging guerrilla warfare and drawing soviet forces further into conflict, the abuses committed by both sides intensified. In the year of a conflict, that followed more than 870,000 Afghans were killed, three million were maimed or wounded, a million were internally displaced and over five million were forced to flee the country. (Jackson 7)

Besides outlining the killing maiming, and displacing of Afghan people during the Soviet occupation of Afghanistan, the report also highlights the psychological problems faced by Afghan people during the civil war that followed the withdrawal of Soviet forces from Afghanistan in 1989. It bring to fore how the war affected the lives of Afghan people who are either force to leave their country or live amid fears of blasts and bullets. The report also details loses to infrastructure that badly collapsed and was then hardly restructured due to the ongoing clashes, adding that the standard of life in Afghanistan could never improve as peace could not prevail during the period. The report further illustrates the impact of war in the lives of people due to the war in the following manner, "A whole generation has grown up never having experiencing peace and many Afghans are Struggling to cope with psychological, economic, social and physical ramification of the conflicts past and present" (Jackson 4).

According to the mid-year report(2015) jointly prepared by United Nations Assistance Mission in Afghanistan (UNAMA) and the Human Rights Office, the number of civil casualties has exceeded the record high number that was recorded in 2014. The report recorded 4921 civilian casualties during the first half of 2015; thus documented one percent in 2015; compared to same period in 2014. Commenting on the report, UN High Commission for human rights Zed Arad Al Hussein says; "This report lays bare the heart-rending, prolonged suffering of civilians in Afghanistan, who continue to bear the brunt of the armed conflict and live in insecurity and uncertainty over whether a trip to back, to a tailoring class, to a court room or a wedding party, may be their last" (66).

In such a situation, several writers respond to such extraordinary tragic conditions of the time. Afghan poets and fiction writers are no exception in this regard. The following translated verses from poems in Pashto language by famous Afghan poet, Jamal gives a glimpse of what the survivors of war in this country have been feeling about the state of affairs in their motherland:

A person is searching for the lost limbs of his young brother withered in a bomb blast. What else one can find in this bloody region except sighs. So, please my beloved, bring a light of glittering tear of your eye to my tomb. O God! Please unload these blackened guns forever, so that we can shower flowers in our village. (qtd. In Khalid 62)

Just like the above translated verse lines originally written in Pashto dialect Afghan fiction in English has also been responding to, and portraying the devastation caused by war in Afghanistan. The study also elaborates the trauma caused by the war, adding that memoirs of the war are such intense that it makes many survivors think of committing suicide. These elaborated accounts from these various sources gives the researchers a glimpse of the suffering of Afghan people. Moreover, many disorders connected to trauma experiences, such as mental health problems give a holistic picture of the ravages of war in Afghanistan.

These results are helpful in measuring the extent of destructions that hit the Afghan people. However, the study of fictional narratives which deals with such a trauma, leads researchers and readers into the minds of survivors, letting them know what the survivors of these incidents felt and how they responded to the very incident of trauma. In such a situation, where the people in Afghanistan been hit by the prolonged war and they have experienced related trauma, the study of fictional depiction of these people and their trauma become equally pertinent.

The study is well in place because fictional literature as a means of gaining and broadening cultural intelligence is best comprehended and appreciated when studied within the strategic context of the condition of the people and the related societal realities.

As the literary writers of fiction influence how a society's culture is preserved or changed, particularly when addressing war crimes and psychological trauma, this study examines the Afghan fiction writer in order, in part to capture the reflection and critique of societal realities, and devastating condition of people of Afghanistan. These societal, realities in this case, can be best comprehended through individual accounts of the survivors of the war. The novelist whose work is investigated in this study, while seeing his home and its modern history as a tapestry rent in form by invasion and internal conflicts, act as a cultural proxies between his homeland and his host societies. He serves as a cultural informant for understanding and learning about people experience. He through portraying the trauma filled lives of characters plays an important role for the troubled Afghan civil society.

This study attempts to investigate the idea of a traumatized homeland, a place from where these writers have been displaced and, especially, the narratives of harsh journey undertaken an account of harsh condition in Afghanistan. This collective trauma can be best portrayed through bringing forth the trauma-filled lives of the individual characters. This endeavour sees how the Afghan writers are hunted by the episodes of the Soviet invasions of the Afghanistan in 1979, the rise of Taliban and the migration of millions of Afghans to other countries, ensuing trouble of Afghan peoples due to these problems as portrayed by Hosseini in *The Kite Runner* (2003). This novel has been selected for this study because the incidents and characters in this novel suffer mainly due to war in Afghanistan. Most of the incidents are primarily caused by the war, which is an important variable under investigation in this study. Moreover, the main characters in this novel show the symptoms of a traumatized individual, who represent many Afghan civilians going through trauma of war in their country. Thus, the selection of this novel for the proposed study has been carried out after proper perusal of the text through the yardstick of the fact if the text caters for war trauma and history.

The analysis of the novel is carried out, keeping in view the model for engaging with trauma that seeks to work through the overwhelming events_ a process which involves acknowledging and transforming legacy of trauma while trying to leave its debilitating effects behind. The study, thus, focuses on how the characters come to terms with the shattering experiences by which they are deeply marked. The events described in this novel are not historical accounts by any means; yet this novel is important public forum in as much as they encourage the empathy of the readers by illustrating the effects of war on survivors, there by carry out the ethical tasks of preserving the vanished and often disavowed moments of Afghans history. In order to carry out the analysis of the novel an overview to trauma has been given in chapter second of this book.

Objectives

The main objective of this study is to investigate the relationship between, trauma fiction and history, with special reference to the fictional portrayal of war in Afghanistan. Following the pattern by trauma fiction that covers mainly the accounts of the Holocaust survivors and/ or the incident of 9/11, the purpose of this study is to analyze the select Afghan fiction in English in the light of trauma literary theory to investigate the individual accounts of the survivors of war in Afghanistan.

One of the objectives of the study is to carry out a detailed study of trauma and PTSD in this vein, the study aims at studying the works of influential theorists in the field of trauma theory such as Cathy Caruth, LaCapra, Freud, Herman and Whitehead to see how they defined and explained trauma. More importantly, the study makes an endeavour to see how Caruth linked this purely psychological concept with history. The study aims to use the same link between trauma and history to study the characters in the novel under discussion.

This study project also studies and records the contributions by other noted writers like Shoshanna Felman, Dory Laub, Kali Tal, Ann whitehead and others. The study aims to discuss and bring forth the pertinent points of these writers in a bid to analyze the select work by Afghan writer.

The study endeavours to see if the individual accounts of the survivors of war and their trauma, as portrayed in the selected Afghan fiction in English are in accordance with the various aspects of trauma literary theory and its tenets as outlined by the above mentioned critics. This study further aims at endeavouring to see if the individual accounts of trauma are individuals only, or they, just like the accounts of the Holocaust survivors, can be applied to the Afghan society as a whole, leading to show the individual trauma as a collective trauma. Moreover, this study endeavours to see, if, following Caruth's footsteps, the survivors accounts, as portrayed in the selected novel can be taken as of some historical significance in terms of the truth value that these accounts carry.

One of the objectives is to see how the characters in the selected novel cope with the trauma of war. Various coping mechanisms such as the one represented by Kai Erikson, Dominic LaCapra and Judith Lewis Herman's have been used to see if the coping with trauma strategies used by the characters as well as their reactions to the overwhelming nature of trauma are in accordance with the models which are recommended by the above mentioned writers. This analysis of the coping strategies used by the characters is helpful in establishing how realistically the characters and their trauma has been portrayed by the novelist; thus enabling the study to see if the witness accounts of trauma as verbalized by the characters can qualify for maintaining any truth value to augment the related history.

Before carrying out the analysis of selected fiction novel, the study aims to carry out a detailed investigation into the work done in the field of trauma fiction in a bid to able to bring this study par with the research carried out in other parts of the world. The study aims at taking a step ahead of the endeavours that investigated the trauma of fictional characters belonging to the Holocaust, the Vietnam war and the 9/11 issues by expanding the range of trauma literary theory and related investigation to the incidents of trauma in countries like Afghanistan. The details of studies, which have been carried out by other researchers to cater for fictional representation of trauma in other parts of the world, have been provided in the literature review in chapter second.

Research Questions

In critical exploration of the text selected for the study with reference to war trauma, history and fiction, thy study tries to address the subsequent significant questions.

Keeping in view of the concepts of acting out and working through in trauma theory, how do the traumatized characters in the selected narrative in English articulate their witnessing of trauma, what measure do the traumatized characters take to keep with the overwhelming incident of war in order to recover from the trauma and reconnect to everyday life?

In what ways can the trauma of the individual characters in the selected novel be ascribed to the collective trauma of Afghan society as a whole, and how does this narrativization of their accounts highlights the collective war-ravages in the Afghan society?

Following Cathy Caruth's footsteps can the portrayal of trauma of the individual characters in the selected novel add something to the history which is recorded under the traditional documented evidence?

Delimitation

It is important to identify delimitation in order to assure the validity of any research work. This study focuses on the characters reaction to overwhelming nature of the incident of war, their coping mechanisms, and the nature of their trauma as either individual, collective or both.

The study pays special attention to see how these accounts, by the surviving characters who witnessed the war, can, in the light of trauma literary theory, qualify for augmenting history due to their truth value.

Significance of the Study

Fictional narratives are rich source of information and, especially for those who do not have firsthand experience with indigenous people. As Richter in his research work entitled, *"Persuasive Effects of Fictional Narratives Increase over Time"* published in an international Journal Media Psychology in (2007) asserts that, "narratives has an implicit influence on the way people view the world as well as shifting people worldwide" (Richter 62). Yet one is left to wonder how the popular fictional narratives in English represent the Afghan people to the western readers, who rely on their outlets as the first hand source of information, and the question remains whether this sort of mass media device reproduces what the western news media represents or if it depicts the Afghan people and their trauma differently.

Tracing the war trauma of the country like Afghanistan, which is not a developed or technological advanced as most of the European and American countries are, brings to attention the fact that just like the Holocaust, the Vietnam War and 9/11, the trauma of Afghan people also hurts. The people in Afghanistan and other such war-hit countries as well as their related traumas require as much attention as do the people in the technologically advanced countries, because what is common among people throughout the world is fact that they feel the same feelings when confronted with trauma of one sort or other. The study is vital in its message that one person's trauma should be felt by his/her fellow beings, no matter where s/he from and no matter what his/her location is, because as Cathy Caruth in her most influential theoretical work *Unclaimed Experience: Trauma Narrative and History* published in (1996) says that, "people all over the world are implicated in each other's trauma" (Caruth 24).

Apart from bringing forth the basics of trauma theory as well as its link to history and fiction, the study is equally useful for understanding the various modes of coping mechanisms as put forward by Judith Lewis Herman, Kai Erikson and Miller. LaCapra's concepts of acting out and working through are useful in understanding the reactions of a trauma victim. These models are explained through character analysis of the novel in terms of their reaction to trauma. This explanation of models and their application on characters in the select novel is of great help for perspective researchers, who can study these models and use any of the models to carry out their analysis of trauma-hit characters in their research.

This study is equally significant in arousing interest among, and encouraging other researchers to entrust themselves with working on literary production of other writers from Afghanistan as well as from other countries, which have been faced with the curse of terrorism. This endeavour encourages other researchers to look for the aftermaths of natural disasters as portrayed in literature and carry out a trauma analysis of these works. A brief discussion on trauma literary theory, trauma symptoms as well as mechanisms for coping with trauma covered in this book in an attempt which greatly help the researchers in the near future, in the countries where unlike developed west, work on literary trauma theory and helps to direct and guide on how to deal with a literary work with reference to this literary theoretical framework.

Chapter division of the study

The first chapter of this book provides an introduction to the study by presenting the background and rationale of the endeavour. The study, first of all, contextualizes the research by briefly providing the impact of the recent wars in Afghanistan and highlighting the problems of the inhabitants of this war-ravaged country. Here, the study draws an analogy between the trauma of technologically advanced countries which went through the troubles of events like Holocaust, the Vietnam war, the 9/11 issues and the trauma of the people of Afghanistan, necessitating the argument that an investigation into the fictional representation of the trauma-hit lives of Afghan people is as in place as that of other developed nations. The chapter outlines the characteristics of trauma of trauma fiction and its relationship with history as mentioned in the works of writers like Cathy Caruth, Dominic LaCapra, Kali Tal, Ann Whitehead and others. The chapter also provides the thesis statement, objectives, significance and delimitation of the study.

The second chapter of this book titled Trauma: An Overview highlights the main theorist in the field of trauma theory. The basic concept of the trauma and the debates involved in this field are also included. Moreover, the study incorporates the place of history in this whole discussion and relates the record of trauma narratives in this discipline. The works of most eminent theorist in this field of trauma such as Cathy Caruth, Dominic LaCapra, Shoshanna Felman Judith Lewis Herman, and others come under discussion in this part. A part from these accounts/discussion on these works, the study refers to the use of these theories in research works, which investigates fictional characters of narratives related to other catastrophic events such as Holocaust, the Vietnam war and 9/11 etc. this part of the study also files a good deal of research that has been carried out on fictional narratives, which are based on the incidents of trauma. This portion of the book highlights the various aspects of the trauma theory which has been used by the several researchers.

The third chapter of this book outlines the models and works of Freud, Caruth, LaCapra, Laub, and Craps and their reference to the history in relation to trauma. This chapter also incorporated with the understanding of trauma with special reference to time and space.

The fourth chapter of the book brings forth the traumatic events as described by Hosseini in the novel *The Kite Runner.* Here the study pays special attention to all the tenets of trauma theory as outlined by the aforementioned writers to see if the reactions and coping with trauma strategies of the individual characters, which went through the trauma, are in accordance with what the theorist in the field of trauma have put forth. This chapter also discusses in detail the novel to look for the ways how the novelist articulate traumatic incidents through the characters and what historical value these accounts carry. This part tries to achieve the objectives and look for answers to the questions which have mentioned in the introductory part of the book.

The fifth and the last chapter of this book titled, Conclusions and Findings, provide answers to the research questions, outlined in the introduction part of the book. Here the study highlights the result and findings of the whole effort to see if the research questions, mentioned in the first chapter, have been answered. In the light of these findings, the study suggests recommendations for perspective researchers in the field. These recommendations are supported by findings, which are based on the study.

CHAPTER TWO

TRAUMA: AN OVERVIEW

According to Merriam Webster Dictionary, Trauma is a Greek word which means "wound". Although the Greeks used the term only for physical injuries, but with the development in trauma theories in the present scenario the word has refers not only to physical injuries but also to the emotional injuries/wounds. Because traumatic events can leave psychological symptoms long after any physical injuries have healed. The psychological reaction to emotional trauma now has an established name: post-traumatic stress disorder, or PTSD. It usually occurs after an extremely stressful event, such as war time combat, a natural disasters, or sexual or physical abuse; its symptoms include depression, anxiety, flashbacks, and recurring nightmares as a result of which the person suffering is unable to get out of the overwhelming nature of event and unable to reconnect temselves to normal live.

As the word is originated from the Greek, but with the emerging trends many theorists have tried to modify the concept to readers and the word does not remain stuck to its limited concept but expands its boundaries. As Jean

Laplanche a French author and Psychoanalyst in his book *The Language of Psychoanalysis* published in translation form by Donald Nicholson Smith in (1974), asserts that:

Trauma: an event in the subject's life is defined by its intensity, by the subject's incapacity to respond adequately to it, and by the upheaval and long lasting effect that it brings about in the physical organization. (Laplanche 4)

Basel van der Kolk, an American psychiatrist and researcher in his book *Psychological Trauma* published in (1987), come forth with the modification and says that:

The essence of psychological trauma is the loss of faith that there is order and continuity in life. Trauma occurs when one loses the sense of having a safe place to retreat within or outside oneself to deal with frightening emotions or experiences. (Van der Kolk 12)

However, the first ever examination of trauma started with the investigation into the concept of hysteria at Paris Hospital (La Salpetriere) with French neurologist Jean-Martin Charcot, with whom Sigmund Freud and Pierre Janet studied in 1880s (Herman 92). Freud's letters which he wrote to his colleague Wilhelm Fliess in 1887 and 1897, indicates that this concept of *Nachtraglichkeit* came to the fore at the same time when the seduction theory of neurosis was developed. According to these trauma theories by Frued that he developed while treating his female patients for hysteria, and for which he used the term Nachtraglichkeit in part second of his book "Project for a Scientific Psychology" that was published posthumously in 1950, he says, "We invariably find that a memory is repressed which has only become a trauma by *deferred action*" [italics in original] (Freud, 33).

This 'delayed reaction' phenomenon in trauma came under investigation and has been discussed by many researchers an number of empirical studies, which were carried in this field also endorsed the value and importance of this deferred action. Moreover, according to the reports from the American Psychiatric Association, published form 1987-2013 after a comprehensive analysis came to the conclusion that, " average 38.2% and 15% of post-traumatic stress disorder PTSD cases in military and civilians sample, respectively have proved to come up with delayed reactions after they were hit by trauma" (Andrews et al 72). It is also pertinent to mention here that an individual's experience that s/he undergoes right after an incident does not qualify him/her for being traumatized until the given conditions are fulfilled (67).

However, the first ever explanation that came before all was that of Sigmund Freud's work *Studies on Hysteria* originally published in (1895) where in it he asserted that " An effect that is created by the memory of a unpleasant incident is simply unavailable when the incident takes place, adding that the memory of incident arouses an effect with a completely new understanding of the incident that has taken place in the past"(). What he means by this is that the victim of traumatic incident comprehends the traumatic effects of the incident only after some time has passed and the victim has haunted by the trauma when he remembers that incidents and encounters the trauma for the second time.

Freud theory of Nachtraglichkeit that was published in his co-authored book with Joseph Breuer with the title *Studies on Hysteria* (1895), he termed the concept as 'retention hysteria'. They explained it as a kind of disorder in the memory, adding that this physical trauma works like a foreign agent in the mind. They further asserted that:

It is not as if it is some kind of symptom or question of the repetition of an action; the whole unpleasant experience is saved in the mind and the whole incident reoccurs as soon as the incident similar to the ones experienced by the victims.()

This gap between the actual incident and its reoccurrence is, as Freud terms it incubation. Freud and Breuer in the book *Study on Hysteria* holds that "as soon as the affected person starts talking about the incident and verbalize the feelings, the symptoms and the overall grip of the incident starts to disappear"().

The issue of latency and the whole concept of trauma theory came to Freud's findings after he dealt with the case history of Katharina. In this case Freud came to know that Katharina had seen her father in bed with her cousin, after which she was suffering from feelings of hatred, disgust and anxiety attacks. She was unaware of why she was having anxiety attacks with such intensity. However, after getting counselling and treatment from Freud, she revealed that she at the age of fourteen went through the unpleasant experience of being sexually assaulted by her father. Freud writes about Katharina's feeling after she revealed this incident, that she felt lively, exalted and relaxed after telling him about the incident. After that, Freud says that Katharina was having the anxiety attacks because that incident had remained her of the traumatic experience that she herself had gone through in the past. So, Freud and his colleague gave several insights related to trauma studies after investigating the case of Katharina.

It was not until 1980s that trauma, related mainly to combat veterans, was investigated, discussed and taken into consideration. However, in the year 1980, the year that is known for making the birth of modern trauma studies,

American Psychiatric Association (APA) acknowledged and included Post Traumatic Stress Disorder (PTSD) in its official *Diagnostic and Statistics Manual* (DSM-III). The contemporary trauma studies got this recognition mainly due to the problems faced by the veterans of war in Vietnam. Later on, noted psychiatrists such as Judith Lewis Herman in her famous work *Trauma and Recovery: From Domestic Abuse to Political Terror* (1992), made an attempt to include, exclusively combat related disorder, other forms of traumas caused by terrorism, war, domestic and sexual violence. From then, on the contemporary trauma studies has been having a more inclusive approach towards trauma and PTSD as it brought together hitherto separated experiences of trauma, caused by domestic and sexual violence, war and terrorism etc. Herman in her book *Trauma and Recovery: Aftermath of Violence from Domestic Abuse to Political Terror* published in (1994) declares that "the investigation into the war trauma and sexual trauma follows the same trajectory if considered their journey in the past" (Herman 63). She further says that "war trauma in the context of world war I was studied as a war neurosis or shell-shock, adding that it was replaced by the PTSD during studies concerning the Vietnam War veterans"(77).

Outlining the main symptoms of PTSD, Davison, Neale and Kring (2004) provide a comprehensive account of the disorder. They say that the survivor, first of all, re-experiences the trauma through nightmares related to the traumatic experience, adding that this flashback can also in the form of various forms of stimuli that remind the survivor of trauma about the incident that s/he has witnessed. They assert that the survivor can be reminded of the traumatic experience through stimuli such as places, smells and sounds, which are associated to the actual traumatic experience. Further they say that as the stimuli have a very negative impact on the survivor, s/he avoid it, which ultimately leads to manifest avoidance, which is the second stage of PTSD. The third stage that they highlight is the loss of memory. Here, the survivor's behaviour of avoidance towards the stimuli can cause the feeling of detachment from one's self and others, thus causing the survivor to lose the detailed memory of the incident of trauma. The fourth and the last stage, according to the writers is that the survivor experiences an increased alertness, problems with sleep, manifest startle response, and an increased emotional and physical arousal. They assert that the survivor may also suffer from the problems of depression, anxiety and the survivor's guilt.

However, Judith Lewis Herman in her book *Trauma and Recovery* (1992), says that:

The biggest impact of psychological trauma is that it shatters one's identity through its pervasiveness and uncontrollability. The exposure of the incident is so much beyond the human usual experience that the victim of trauma suffers damage to the basic structure of the self. (Herman 96)

In the similar fashion Dominic Labara in her most notable theoretical work *Writing History, writing Trauma* published in (2001), says that the main characteristics of trauma is that it breaks the self apart during the whole process(LaCapra 29-30). This happens because what characterize a trauma is the fact that the fundamental assumptions of the sense of control of one's self and safety are taken away, leaving the victim with a shaken trust in him/herself and his/her surroundings. In this manner trauma not only shakes the victim's trust in themselves but it also effects his/her relations with people living around themselves.

In the same vein as Herman in *Trauma and Recovery: Aftermath of Violence from Domestic Abuse to Political Terror* (1992), explains in detail the impact of trauma as she says that:

The impact of trauma is so huge that it compromises the victim's trust in self and others. On the one hand, trauma compels the victim to stay aloof from people living around him/her, while, on the other hand it also makes him/her depend on them, thus placing the victim in a state of utter confusion. As a result, the trauma victim's behaviour towards people around him/her turns unusual and unstable that is marked by contradictory things like intimacy at one time and complete detachment at another. (Herman 154)

Thus trauma came into existence as a theory. In other words, with its wrapped temporality and inquisitive structural expression, psychic trauma caters for the re-enactment of experiences, which went missing from getting recorded at the time when incident took place. The very history of trauma theory is termed as what Herman, in her book *Trauma and Recovery* (1992), puts it, as that of episodic amnesia because this has time and again guided researchers and critics into realms, which were considered as unthinkable in the past. She adds that denial, dissociation and repression have, since long, been considered as essential parts of individual as well as the social conscious and that trauma theory is related to addressing the complication arising from this phenomenon. On the same note Kali Tal in his *Worlds of Hurt: Reading the Literature of Trauma* (1996), observes that "the penalty on social as well as individual level of this act of repression is repetition, which in trauma theory is termed as flashback and acting out etc (Tal 88). It becomes clear that outing trauma incident in the framework of history cannot separate theory and events from each other. Cathy caruth in her book *Unclaimed Experience: writing History Writing Trauma* (1995), highlights the same phenomenon in the following words:

Once the notion of traumatic temporality has been introduced, longer simply possible to place this notion with in a larger and more traditional temporal framework (that is to place the conceptual event of theory of trauma within the framework of the empirical, institutional, and cultural histories that are its contexts), since that would disavow the central insight of the theory, which suggests that our more traditional conceptual histories may have to be rethought. (Caruth 19)

Caruth while explaining the phenomenon between theory and trauma, asserts that history re-enters theory in temporal conception of trauma. Drawing from Freud, as she discusses the inseparability of the theorization of trauma and its history, Caruth emphasizes that Freud (1895), while trying to escape the neurosis, accidently meets Katharina (as mentioned before), takes on her all-important case study, suggesting, the words of Freud himself, "as if theory itself emerged as the interruption of forgetting."

Thus, as the victim of trauma is hit by the memories of the incident long after the threat has been vanished; similarly the investigation into trauma is usually not carried out at the moment of the traumatic incident but after sometime, when the conventional method of recording events, namely, history, fails to grasp intensity of the shocks felt by the victims. Thus trauma emerged as an event that was not recognised the way it should have been until it repeatedly returned with greater impetus through literary productions, historical events and political studies. This theory related background to trauma leads us to representation of trauma in literary productions.

An upsurge of publication has been visible in the field of psychological trauma and its representation in literature during the last few decades or so, mainly concerning and depicting events which cannot be grasped and depicted through historical accounts. The mostly traumatized world that provides a great deal of subject matter to cater for in the fields of the Holocaust studies, art, science, law, psychiatry, literature and historiography, the unison of literature and trauma attempts to investigates how these untellable stories are represented and what aspects, which went missing from the historical accounts, are highlighted. Such is the extreme and unusual nature of the concept of representation in these events that it geared up researchers for their great interest in trauma studies during the last few decades.

This need for the new concept of representation led to huge number of publication of trauma narratives in fictional as well as non-fictional streams after the works on contemporary trauma theory by literary scholars such as Cathy Caruth, Shoshanna Felman, and Geoffrey Hartman in 1990s. As a result of this emergence of literary trauma theory, the importance of the relationship of literature and trauma grew manifold.

The reference of trauma through literature comes under scrutiny for a start due to the curious spatiotemporal structure of trauma that cannot be represented through the traditional way of representation. The question that inevitably comes to the mind regarding this representation of trauma through literature is how literature can represent trauma when trauma resists narrativization due to its incomprehensibility upon occurrence. As Caruth once again gave explanation to the question in her most familiar work Unclaimed Experience: Writing History Writing Trauma (1995), where in it she asserts, "that trauma eschews being recorded through the language"(Capra 23). It means that it cannot be represented in any form that is linguistically recognised. However, Caruth further explains this representbility issue that although trauma cannot be expressed upon occurrence but it does not mean that its references should be ruled out altogether. She adds that the victim's experience of the incident of trauma is termed an unclaimed experience because it is inherently unrepresentable due to its disruptive referentiality. Caruth's explanation of the phenomenon is in line with that of Dory Laub and Shoshanna Felman who in their book titled *Testimony: Crisis Witenessing the Literature of Trauma* published in 1992 says, according to whom the survivor's failure or inability to make sense of the events lies at the base of trauma. They argue that:

Trauma survivors live not with the memories of the past, but with an event that could not and did not proceed through to its completion, has no ending, attained no closure, and therefore, as for as its survivors are concerned, continues into the present and is current in every respect. The survivor indeed, is not truly in touch with either the core of his traumatic reality or with the fatedness of its re-enactments, and thereby remains entrapped in both. (Laub Felman 69)

Thus, the trauma survivor remains trapped in the moment of the incident and simply cannot move on. The severity of the incident and its ensuing impact is so intense that the survivor is unable to bring the incident to an end in his mind, even when the actual incident has already gone past. So Kali Tal in his book World of Hurts: Reading the literature of Trauma says that "these flashbacks and haunting of this incident continue to hover around the survivor and keep the incident as fresh and untainted his/her mind as recording on a videotape" (Tal 7).

CHAPTER THREE

UNDERSTANDING TRAUMA WITH RESPECT TO SPACE AND TIME

The main focus of this part of the study is on the notions of space and time as well as their impact on trauma. This is the approach that resulted from the recommendations given by Caruth (1992), who advises this method for reading and discovering better approaches to cater for trauma and its impact. This section of the study expects to add to the scholarly trauma research by using the concepts of time and space to rethink and grow to the thought of speaking to and reading trauma, other than the models discussed in the previous chapter of the study. This portion of the study is based on the tenets of trauma theory that has been put forward by Cathy Caruth, as discussed earlier. Now, before discussing Hosseini's *The Kite Runner* what this part of the study does is that it, in order to bring to fore the concepts of time and space with reference to trauma, takes into consideration 'Gerusalemme Liberata' (Jerusalem Delivered) and its two scenes by Tasso. This discussion then, goes on to study the selected novel for the study in the vein of same theoretical frame.

In the introduction to her *Unclaimed Experience: Trauma Narrative and History* (1996), Caruth begins her interpretation of another method of perusing trauma by returning to Freud's composition in section three of "Beyond the Pleasure Principle" (1920), to discuss two passages from Tasso's romantic epic of Tancredo and Clorinda. She discusses the demonic way of representation of trauma in perpetual repetition, or the death drive, Freud compresses the two scenes of Gerusalemme story. Which recounts the account of the attack of Jerusalem by the Christians in their first campaign in 1099 and the fights between the Christians and the Muslims as caruth introduced the event from Freud's book as:

The hero Tancred unwittingly kills his beloved Clarinda, She having done battle with him in the disguise armor of an enemy knight. After her burial he penetrates the strange charmed forest that so frightens the army of crusaders, There he smites a tall tree with his sword, the blood gushes from the wound and the voice of Clarinda, whose spirit has magically entered into the very tree, accuses him of yet again doing harm to his beloved. (Freud 16)

As indicated by Freud, Tancred's twofold injuring of his beloved has been done unknowingly, first in the battling, where he doesn't recognizes her shield, and afterwards in the forested area, where she is buried in tree and misrecognizes once more, reveals insight into the impulse to repeat in traumatic despondency, by an apparently secretive power, i.e. power for which the rationale is oblivious and can't without much of a stretch be discovered. Tancred thus, unwittingly reorders the traumatic moment. Tancred's unknowing wound of Clorinda demonstrates the inert impulsive nature of traumatic reiteration, in which the damaged people unwittingly are compelled to belatedly come back to the trauma just as "a daemonic current [is] going through their whole existence" (Freud 87).

Like Freud Caruth in her discourse on trauma framework, concentrates on Tancred's experience of the transient way of trauma, which cannot be grasped at the moment of occurrence; however, which must be repeated later, yet while she sees in Tasso's story[the] most moving poetical portrayal of "an interminable redundancy of the same destiny" (Caruth 60). She sees Tasso's account likewise as a "striking" example of "the moving voice that shouts out, a voice that is incomprehensibly discharged through the trauma" (Caruth 2). At the end of the day, Caruth emphasizes the moral basic of trauma in delayed setting created by the expression.

In Caruth's examination, the voice from the trauma vouches for the "reality or truth" of the trauma that has gotten away from Tancred's awareness and speaks to that which is blocked off in some other way, directing the reader's listening and seeing. She says:

the address of the voice[...] as the story of the way in which one's own trauma is tied up with the trauma of another, the way in which trauma may lead, therefore, to the encounter with another, through the very possibility and surprise of listening to another's wound.(Caruth 4-8)

As it were, Clorinda vouches for what Tancred can't recollect or know, thus rises as his double. The reader is then thrown in the part of the victimized person and witness, dissolving the limits in the middle of time and space, self and other, so the trauma can't be situated in any one individual or place yet rather is exchanged to interlock with, or implicates, every one of us.

In spite of the fact that Caruth in her Unclaimed Experience: Trauma Narrative and History (1996), comments in her explanation that Tasso's account seems to light up not simply the worldly but "both the temporal and spatial aspects of the notion of trauma" (Caruth 114). Thus a point worth noting is that she doesn't keep on contemplating on this connection in the middle of time and space in trauma or endeavor to characterize spatiality in a traumatic setting any further in her book. it is true that the cited entry above shows both the temporal and spatial parts of trauma yet she neglects to address issues raised by the connection between these in Tasso's story and does not thoroughly consider the ramifications of this connection for comprehension of trauma and its representation. Nor does her new method of perusing propose how trauma can be investigated regarding space.

Consequently, the inquiries concerning why psychic trauma needs to be theorized, spoken to, and read through both time and space remain generally unaddressed and unexplored in her hypothesis. This study perceives and addresses this oversight or blind side and is dedicated to seeking after this issue, which appears to be critical to a comprehension of trauma and its representation, offering a marginally diverse problem by broadening the idea of space in this setting.

Beginning from Caruth's and Freud's insights about the disengagement that is in alienable in traumatic experience, this chapter recommends that references to time and space picture the traumatized personality, flagging the twofold way if traumatic experiences as well as bespeaking thus the delicacy of our impression of these ideas even with trauma. Since these references signals towards a psychological part in trauma, they ought not be conjectured, read separately or translated independently. Rather, it is important to reevaluate their connection, through the issue of trauma, to characterize trauma through this connection, and to figure out how to read trauma for interruptions and dislocations regarding these transient and spatial references separately.

Aside from lighting up complex and a multifaceted worldly structure in traumatic repetition, what emerges about this entry in Tasso's story is likewise how it shows a spatial side to trauma notwithstanding the fleeting in a more extensive sense than topping off the space of the brain – even a material, physical or mortal angle – to traumatic memory and enduring with gendered ramifications: the rough scene of the first killing of Clorinda in the twelfth of the twenty cantos in Tasso's epic underscores the space of her body, and is itself suggestive of sexual viciousness, not a phenomenal "weapon" of war.

Caruth's comprehension of the spatial measurement of trauma is centered around the brain, nonetheless, and gets to some degree from Jean Laplanche, who underscores the route, in which Freud places the worldly story close to a spatial one that is not spatial in the physical sense but instead about expansion and borrowed from Jacques Derrida, who recommends that in Freud a geological structure is fundamental to the likelihood of a file (as the likelihood of memory) (Caruth 97)

Trauma and Identity

Memory negotiates the connection between trauma and identity. Trauma is closely joined with memory due to the fact that it is due to the memory of an incident that trauma occurs. As Luckhurst in his book *The Trauma*

Question (2008), states that "other than a bunch of physical implications, trauma disturbs memory, and consequently the identity of the victims, in exceptional ways" (Luckhurst 134). Dory Laub in his *Testimony: Crisis of Witnessing in Literature, Psychoanalysis and History* (1992), concentrates on the effect of trauma on memory and thus, the impact of memory on the victim's comprehension of trauma. His theory is created from his work with Holocaust survivors, where he concentrates on the victim's shifts of knowing and not knowing the traumatic incident. Trauma is seen as an occasion that is not that is not completely grasped by the brain and consequently stays outside its typical working. Then again, it does have a very basic impact in the individual's life as it returns regularly in a literal as well as comprehensive manner.

The victim of trauma may relive the very trauma but without the ability to connect with it; it is both known and unknown to the individual. In his investigation of different conditions of known damage to the mind, Laub distinguishes eight types of traumatic knowledge, for example fragments (decontextualized memories), overpowering narratives (the narrator is overtaken by a memory that obscures the present), not knowing (amnesia), witness narratives (distance and perspective is obtained), and fugue states (intrusive appearance of fragmented behavior, cognitions and effects). The different manifestations of traumatic knowledge as shown above are also the well-known trauma symptoms. For example, the dissociated image of an incident of trauma may hunt the victim in the form of flashbacks. Knowing and not knowing trauma is focal as in the individual can't really understand the experience and express it in words it to endure witness to the occasion, some of the time not even to him/herself.

This division of the self into a known and unknown part slices to the very center of the individual's perception toward self and identity.

Caruth further clarifies this by recommending that an individual conveys, "an impossible history within them, or they become themselves symptoms of the history that they cannot entirely posses" (Caruth 5).

It is exactly her attention to the history and the particular incident that prompts Radstone and Leys to differ with Caruth's trauma theory. Despite this, it does highlight the complex relationship of the self to history that is at the focal point of traumatic experience. In the meantime, turning into a mere symptom of history may also strip the single person of organization and dangers undermining the hallmarks of the essence of an individual.

Radstone further proposes that by withdrawing from the processes of the unconscious and concentrating on the incident as the focal point, Cruth et al. disregard two essential certainties: that inside the unconscious there is no division between the normal and the pathological obsessive, and that the darkness not only cones from outside but it also resides inside the psyche itself. Thus, she proposes to substitute a fully passive yet sovereign subject with someone who is hit by circumstances in a way that all his conscious cannot grasp everything therein. Yet even this movement does not totally evade the idea of the split self, as contends that there is a perspective that cannot be known inside trauma, regardless of the fact that he unknowable part is not an event but a process of the unconscious.

This multiplying of the self into two in terms of a difficult to reach trauma and the self is likewise taken up by Robert Jay Lifton. In a meeting with caruth, he clarifies that intense trauma shatters one's sense of self to a great extent, adding that there a new traumatized self is created. Critics, analysts and writers demonstrate that this parting of the self happens in the survivor's memory and the best way to mend from trauma is to asserts, "So the battle in the post-traumatic experience is to reconstitute the self into the single self, reintegrate itself."

This reconstitution of the traumatized self happens through testimony where the survivor endeavors to make a reasonable narrative of the past with the assistance of a listener or a witness. Radstone in *"Trauma Theory: Contexts, Politics, Ethics"* proposes that this is the externalization of the internal meaning making that happens inside the psyche "a model of subjectivity grounded in the space between witness and testifier inside which that which can't be known can start to be witnessed" (Radstone 20).

It is exactly this space between witness and testifier that is the main area of investigation in this study, mainly because this is the place where language and fictional narratives become the focal points in creating identity and history with reference the particular incident of traumatic nature.

In the meantime as an integrative story must be made with the goal that recuperation should happen, a narrative additionally needs to show different contending and on occasion conflicting strands- one of which is exactly the knowing and not-knowing of the trauma. The self accordingly gets to be dependent on an account; a methodology that is near to Ricoeur's reasoning around the self, story, and time, Which he provided in *Time and Narrative* (1988). Luckhurst also uses Ricoeur's thought of "concordant dissonance" to propose a route in which the story can speak of trauma. This perspective is near to Weine's contention, according to which testimony is polyphonic in nature. Weine further recommends that a survivor could be seen regarding Bakhtin's idea of Dostoevsky's hero as somebody who is looking for "self-definition" and who is engrossed with getting to self-conscious. It is through testimony that the individual has the capacity to draw in with both consciousness and the memory of the incident, which as per Weine can best be attained to through a dialogic and polyphonic account:

In polyphonic and dialogic testimony it is the elaboration, not the erasure, of the picture that is the important element. [...] it is also essential that this elaboration not stop at some boundary just outside of the self, and fail to consider broader social, cultural, spiritual, development, and ethic concerns and struggles. Amore elaborated story may help the survivor to grow in terms of his or her consciousness and ethics. (Bakhtin 104)

Testimony is therefore both an entrance point to trauma and memory, and a pathway to mending. It is through narrative that the self is made and re-made. For Weine's testimony facilitates the development and growth of comprehending the incident in all its forms and manifestations. Besides, the joining of different historical, ethical, communal and social perspectives permits the individual to see themselves as more than simply a victim of trauma, and to see their trauma in a more extensive setting.

Regarding the Afghan experience of the trauma of War, additionally considers the impact of the predominant individual perspective, which has been neglected by studies so far. Studies in subjectivity indicate how individuals were endeavoring to make their characters through expanding their progressive cognizance in narratives. In the same way, the witness endeavors to accommodate the self and the character with its connection to trauma. Weine's and Ricoeur's perspective of narrative along these lines takes into account the reconciliation of these different perspectives without abandoning the account as a particular impression of trauma.

Trauma and Unspeakability

One of the biggest obstacles to making a narrative and subsequently a stable identity is the rupture of the individual perception of time and memory that the injury is caused by an incident of trauma. As recommended by Laub, traumatic memory is fragmented and internal, always interfering with an individual's experience of time and life. Besides, this memory is voluntary but not accessible, as Caruth in *Trauma Exploration in Memory* (1995), says, that "The ability to recover the past is thus closely and paradoxically tied up, in trauma, with the inability to have access to it" (Caruth 152). So, narrative has to cater for representing this relationship of knowing and not knowing the memory of an incident of trauma along with its impact on the victim. Laub says that the putting into words of a traumatic incident is vital to understand the incident and making the healing possible, adding that:

Much of knowing is dependent on language [...] Because of the radical break between trauma and culture, victims often cannot find categories of thought or words for their experience. That is, since neither culture nor experience provides structures for formulating acts of massive aggression, survivors cannot articulate trauma, even to themselves. (Laub 288)

On account of this absence of structures through which to speak trauma, it is frequently portrayed as unrepresentable, unspeakable and that it is experienced as an absence. However, this appears differently in relation to the consistent reiteration of the traumatic occasion in the form of fragments of intrusive memory and the literal form of that memory. This is exactly what Caruth investigates in her work by studying the complex ways that knowing and not knowing are caught in the language of trauma and in the stories connected with it. Using Freud's sample of Tasso's "Tancred and Clorinda" she proposes that trauma is not locatable in the basic brutal or unique occasion in a victim's past, yet rather in the way that its extremely unassimilated nature comes back to haunt the survivor later on. This unassimilated nature can be associated with Radstone's clarification of the space "in between" where trauma is seen, as opposed to either inside the occasion or totally inside the psyche. At the core of this issue is the conviction that trauma in its most genuine structure may be unrepresentable, as narrative can't join both knowing and not knowing all the while.

Regarding the very notion of un-representability, investigations press hard to look for the three implications of "unspeakable" in reference to Holocaust. That firstly, it is "verbally unrepresentable", secondly, it is "inexpressibly bad", and thirdly, it may not or can't be talked about as a result of the holy nature of the incident. What Trezises brings up is the strain between a real claim based on facts rendered as impossible and a moral prescription against probability, both of which are dominant in the Holocaust related discourse

He demonstrates that the hindrance in talking about the Holocaust is by all accounts the language that seems inadequate to cater for this phenomenon, adding that it recognizes the fact that this insufficiency does not describe the structure in connection to some object that is lying totally outside of it, but that it mirrors the inside rupture of the system by a reality that surpasses its limits. The harm that the incident does to a medium of expression i.e. language is like the way that a traumatic occasion is said to harm the psyche. The interruption is inside the language, as a part of connection to the Holocaust could be seen as if the generally meaningless phenomenon is being burdened with meaning that will ultimately lead to "aesthetic success and ethical failure" (Trezises 45).

On the issue of representing traumatic incident in narratives Kolk and Hart (1995), question if it was not the desecration of traumatic experiences to reconstruct them in narratives, Stories about traumatic encounter are constantly postured against the conviction that to discuss trauma is like betraying it, yet talking it out is proposed as the main cure for the survivors. At the same time, there are times in history that join a few contending narratives, and, as Kelly in his book *Comrade Pavlik: The Rise and the Fall of a Soviet Boy Hero* (2005), recommends, there is evidence of communities which articulated trauma in a very successful manner.

The perspective of the unspeakable trauma is accordingly in peril of undermining traumas that are very much verbalized. It is likewise imperative to call attention to the view that un-speakability may also mean something that has not been spoken of as yet and that it may mean that there was no chance to discuss a particular trauma, which remained unnoticed and silent under several other narratives covering other trauma. Merridale in his "*Amnesiac Nation*" (2005), proposes that "this unspoken perspective is definitely not pathological and in this way can't be seen through the trauma framework of investigation" (Merridale 76). However, silence stands and speaks for some incident and that cannot be disregarded.

To recommend that the representation of trauma is a disloyalty of it would make several incidents of trauma go excluded and unnoticed just because they do not conform to the unspeakability mode of trauma. In the same vein, it is in the domain of literary language to look into and discuss the issue of representation and the impossibility of representation, the knowing and the not-knowing and the inside and the outside of the phenomenon itself.

The reason behind this incursion is that fiction is the only possible answer for this unrepresentability because "the disjunction between experiencing (phenomenal or empirical) and understanding (thoughtful naming, in which words replace things, or their images), is what figurative language express and explores" (Hartman 540). Luckhurst (2008) further explains additionally proposes that, "if trauma is a crisis in representation, then this generate narrative possibility just as much as impossibility, a compulsive outpouring of attempts to formulate narrative knowledge" (Luckhurst 83). Thus, literary or figurative language is obviously not by any means the only way to deal with trauma; however, it is an approach that has the capacity to investigate it from without itself, from alternate points of view that can be made through innovative narratives.

After the aforementioned discussion on trauma with reference to time and space, it is now apt to discuss the selected Afghan fictional narrative with special reference to Hosseini's *The Kite Runner*. A detailed discussion on the trauma of war and the characters reaction to the trauma and their coping mechanisms to trauma as put before the reader by Khalid Hosseini in his debut novel has been discussed in the forthcoming chapter.

CHAPTER FOUR

WAR, TRAUMA AND COPING MECHANISMS IN THE NOVEL

In the first large portion of the novel, Baba is introduced as a colossal pashtun, a power of nature, who is something of a legend with a story that he had once wrestled a dark bear a story no one ever sets out to disbelief. He is big by all accounts assuming the part of a God or an alternate creature with over worldly gimmicks because he is most likely the strongest character, about all-powerful and almost bigger than life. Also, he has to choose "what was dark and what was white" (Hosseini, 14). Who else than the God has the chance to choose about this? It is this God-like nature of his father that is so troublesome for Amir to achieve and fulfill. Other than his qualities and force, Baba is respected for his strength and dauntlessness. Baba is without a doubt a fearless man. Not just in the way that he doesn't demonstrate his trepidation and has the capacity to battle a bear, but he is likewise dominant in a manner that he takes after his dreams and doesn't permit individuals to change them. Actually, while doing something such a great amount of magnanimousness as building a shelter, "he doesn't permit other individuals to change his arrangements and he is not ready to listen to their far-fetched remarks" (Hosseini 12).

There are places in the book, when Baba's boldness can practically make him resemble an extra-ordinary and inconceivable cartoon hero, whose acting is difficult to comprehend for the viewers. This happens for instance when he is ready to confront a Russian soldier with a specific end goal to shield a young lady from being assaulted. Hosseini puts the remarks about Baba as:

The bulldog-faced Russian raised his gun. Baba, sit down, please, I said, tugging at his sleeve. I think, he really means to shoot you. Baba slapped my hand away. Haven't I taught you anything? He snapped. He turned to grinning soldier. Tell him he'd better kill me good with that first shot. Because if I don't go down, I'm tearing him to pieces, goddamn his father! (Hosseini 101)

In this minute, Baba's gallantry is tempered by Amir's aside and makes the scene so much genuine and so justifiable. When it's all said and done, Amir has no one left other than his father and there is the lady's spouse who ought to remain behind her. However, he knows Baba and understands it would not be Baba on the off chance that he would act in an unexpected way. As described by Hosseini as, " Do you always have to be the hero? I thought, my heart fluttering. Can't you just let it go for once? But I knew he couldn't – it wasn't in his nature. The problem was, his nature was going to let us kill all" (Hosseini 101).

However, there are considerably more diverse hues in Baba's valor. He is not just gallant to remain against the strings of different kinds; he is also ready to acknowledge reality, however troublesome it is. All things considered it costs much strength to face the way that his adored nation and home is no more a decent place to live in. He, when faced with leaving all the magnanimousness that he enjoys in Afghanistan, has the much-needed mental strength to *'work through'* the traumatic times. What's more it expresses considerably more determination to take off for a completely strange country, where Baba is no longer going to be an honored legend.

As LaCapra in her book *Writing History, Writing Trauma* (2001) puts it, "the survivor of a traumatic incident should be able to differentiate the traumatic incident from the ordinary life and that he should be able to take the incident as a part of life" (LaCapra 87). Baba, though still haunted by the past grandeur, is going to change. In spite of the fact that, his trademark peculiarities outline, the outside conditions make Baba lose quite a bit of his previous acclaim. Yet, he experiences all with his average strength and wishes to furnish his child with opportunities to live and succeed in a free nation.

This is typical of the coping with trauma mechanism as put forth by Herman in her book *Trauma and Recovery: Domestic Abuse to Political Terror* (1992), says that the survivor, "in order to recover from the impact of trauma, should be able to reconnect to life as soon as possible"(Herman 34). Baba does make an attempt to get out of the overwhelming power of the traumatic incident by making a concerted effort to look beyond this incident and to reconnect to everyday life. He, instead of mourning about his own loss of grandeur, shifts his attention to the better future of his son, as he says; "I didn't bring us here for me, did I? (Hosseini 172).

The impact of this traumatic incident, caused by the war in Afghanistan doesn't cease when he leaves his country; rather as the conditions are changing the relationship of Baba and Amir is changing too. It may be brought on by the climbing significance of Amir for Baba- it is nothing abnormal when worker folks need to depend on their kids. However, as Herman (1992) asserts that the last stage in coping with traumatic mechanism is that the survivor should reconnect to life, Baba, in the same vein, reconnect of life as he starts thinking in terms of the future of his son. Anyhow, all the more presumably, it is created on the grounds that Baba has now a stand out child, to whom he put his trust and wishes. All of a sudden, the profession of an author doesn't appear to be as unimportant, as it has been in Afghanistan and Baba learns at any rate to attempt to comprehend his child. At last, their relationship reaches its climax, when Baba is willing to do something he refused in Kabul that "... he reads Amir's stories" (Hosseini 150).

As Cathy Caruth in *Trauma Exploration in Memory* (1995), asserts that "the survivor of trauma will have memories of his past life that will continue haunting him" (Caruth 167). Baba, due to the fact that the new environment that is not that troublesome for him, continues to experience more flashbacks of his previous force and honor, which are shown by Hosseini now and then in the novel. When he rejects the welfare food stamps and when he orders Amir not to tell anyone about his infection, this is the moment when his past influences his decisions in the present. Being in the present, he still lives in the past when he was enjoying a high position in Kabul. He, in other, is not ready to accept whatever he has been deprived of due to the war in his country. The memories of his rich past still haunt him, not letting him to fore go his identity in this new situation. Thus, he remains true to his values which he holds dear to himself and thus refuses to accept the ration cards in this new country.

The extent of how agonizing it has been for Baba to leave Afghanistan, due to the ravages of war, has been shown by Hosseini the aforementioned account. The same situation has been equally validated by personal narratives of Afghan refugees who left their country. A number of such factual accounts have been provided by Amnesty International in 2012. This project covers the personal narratives of Afghan refugees who left their country and took asylum in Australia. One such Afghan refugee, named Najeeba, speaks out regarding her experience of leaving Afghanistan for good, as she says: "leaving your country for good is one of the hardest decisions you can be forced to make. It means a break with all that you know- your family, your livelihood, your friends. All the familiar, sounds, smells and tastes..." (88).

Another Afghan refugee by the name of Chaman Shah Nasiri gives reasons for why he was compelled to leave his country, relatives and friends, saying that "After I left, my father was tortured so badly that he died in prison. If I have stayed in Afghanistan the same thing would have happened to me" (89). This validation of what Baba says through such personal narratives of factual nature shows that a fiction writer represents what people feel and go through in reality. The instances of the aforementioned factual narratives grant credibility to the fiction under investigation by bringing it closer to reality.

Then again, it ought to be noticed, that these two demonstration are propelled by his bravery as well the more presumably by his need to dependably take care of his honor. He fears that he would lose his respect, regardless of the fact whether he was living in a posh area in Kabul or in an ordinary place anywhere else.

Subsequently, if Baba is agonized over his honor, does he fear likewise something else? The answer is undoubtedly yes. He is all that much concerned with the character of his child, Amir whom he values more than anything else. Hosseini shows the following love between Amir and Baba; Amir and Hassan; Amir's love for his mother, the kite flying adventures of Amir and Hassan, and Amir inability to come to Hassan's help when he was in trouble, in order to tell the reader how full-fledged human beings these characters are. The novelist does this intentionally in order for him to be, later on, able to foreground the intense trauma of war, dislocation, and terror against this background.

Baba has been a valiant and courageous man but, like many other father, he lacks the ability to know his child's inclinations. Amir appears frail to him. There is one and only individual he can impart his stresses to. Furthermore, it is his best and closest companion Rahim Khan, who has the benefit to talk transparently with Baba and remind him of oversights; however, they appear to be so few. He is the one to whom Baba can trust his disappointment with Amir. As depicted by Hosseini as:

-I know, I know. But he is always buried in those books or shuffling around the house like he's lost in some dream.

-And?

-I wasn't like that. Baba sounded frustrated, almost angry.

-Rahim Khan laughed. Children are not coloring books you don't get to fill them with your favorite colors.

-Sometimes I look out of the window and I see him playing on the street with the neighborhood boys. I see how they push him around, take his toys from him, gave him a shove, a whack there. And, you know he never fights back. Never. (Hosseini 19)

However, the war has not deprived him of his lavish lifestyle and first rate citizenship in Afghanistan but there is also more to mourn for Baba. Rahim Khan is the main individual left to uncover to Amir about Baba's mystery and wellspring of his most awful stresses; the mystery of Baba's illegitimate child, Hassan. Having always seen Hassan in front of his eyes and growing up alongside Amir all these years, now the war has deprived him of his illegitimate son as well. He is no more able to see him again and this is what has been adding to his pain.

The reason is that with Hassan, Baba's most exceedingly awful emotions of trepidation are constantly joined. Baba is continually caring for Hassan and treating him as pleasantly as the circumstances permit, he pays him a restorative surgery to conform his parted upper lift, he try to invest just as much time with him as with Amir. He demonstrates a guardian like trepidation for Hassan. Also when Hassan and Ali go out, Amir perceives the amount it moves his father. It is one of the minutes, when even god like Baba is on his knees. The circumstance is stronger than him and he is not ready to change it. The power of the war is so huge that it can tumble this giant like a man, called Baba. It has the power to make him mourn over the loss because as Herman says that the second stage in a survivor of a trauma is mourning over the loss. Baba has survived the war and he has been able to get out of his country but the loss is too big for a strong person like him. It is a fact that he doesn't succumbs to this unusual as well overpowering experience because he has been able to work through it, but the fact remains that it is the beyond-human-exposure nature of the calamity that has made a person like Baba mourn. As Hosseini puts it as:

Then I saw Baba do something I had never seen him do before: He cried. It scared me a little, seeing a grown man sob. Father's were not supposed to cry- please, Baba was saying, but Ali had already turned to the door, Hassan trailing him. I'll never forget the way Baba said that, the pain in his plea, the fear. (Hosseini 93)

At that point, his forceful feelings are justifiable concerning his and Ali's dependable companionship. "This mourning on part of the survivor is the second stage for the survivor of trauma. This act of mourning the losses work like restricting the trauma that the survivor has witnessed" (LaCapra 36).

It is not hard for researchers of trauma studies to envision how Baba must feel when he lives far away from Afghanistan in the security of a democratic state and hears all the news of executions and punishments in Afghanistan. Does he have any news about the other child? There is no confirmation of it, presumably not. He can't help contemplating Hassan because the survivor's guilt is like a two edged sword, where on the one hand the survivor keeps on dreading how he survived the calamity and on the other hand, he keeps on thinking why he survives to carry the burden of having witnessed the troubles of the people to become a prey to the traumatic incident. Baba cannot resist recalling Hassan whom he left in the middle of war in Afghanistan, when he says on the occasion of Amir's birthday:"-rolled his head towards me [Amir]. I wish Hassan had been with us today," he said (Hosseini 116).

The last yet one of the important trademarks of Baba which ought not be overlooked in his ethical disposition and how he sees wrong doings. He responds to Amir's stresses that he is a delinquent when drinking scotch in afterwards:" If there is a God out there, then I would hope he has more important things to attend to than my drinking scotch or eating pork" (Hosseini 16). As he explained:

There is only one sin, only one. And that is theft. Every other sin is a variation of theft. (...) when you kill a man, you steal a life, Baba said. You steal his wife's right to a husband rob his children of a father. When you tell a lie, you steal someone's right to the truth. When you cheat, you steal the right to fairness. Do you see? (Hosseini, 16)

At the point when near to the end of the novel, Baba feels the guilt and considers himself a delinquent who has stolen Amir's sibling, Hassan's father and their entitlement to know reality. It would be excessively simple and poorly considered to see Baba as a negative hero. As his companion Rahim Khan clarifies:"he was a man torn between two parts, Amir Jan: you and Hassan. He cherished you both. Yet he couldn't love Hassan the way he yearned to. (..) when he saw you, he saw himself. What's more his blame? (Hosseini 263). It is clear that the amount Baba was pursued by the trepidation that his child may turn out the same delinquent as he himself. He urgently attempted to maintain a strategic distance from it and brought Amir up as an upright and daring man yet his exertion and requests on Amir's character led on as opposed to Amir's shortcoming and craving to be increased in value by his father which at long last pursued Amir into selling out Hassan. Later on, Amir acknowledges:"As it turned out, Baba and I were more indistinguishable than I'd ever known. We had both double-crossed individuals who would have given their lives for us" (Hosseini 197).

Anyhow, it would not be reasonable to end the depiction of Baba without reminding that he for his entire life attempted to be a decent individual but was badly broken by the trauma of war. The main impetus for this was likely his regret created by his powerlessness to concede Hassan in his childhood. Now, in his old age, he is helpless due to the war in his country. He cannot go back to mend the things that he could not do rightly. At the same time, the thought processes in goodness are not after all so essential, the decency itself is what is important. Rahim Khan concludes:

Once in a while, I think all that he did, nourishing the poor in the city, constructing the orphanage, offering cash to companions in need, it was all his method for making up for himself. Also that, I accept is the thing that genuine recovery is, Amir Jan, when blame prompts goodness. (Hosseini 263)

Also in his quest for recovery, Amir truly ended up being Baba's child. Amir is without a doubt the primary character of *The Kite Runner*. It is his confidence, the readers take after and his wrong doing which is the moving power of the novel. At the outset, the readers are crashed into perusing by yearning to find what is Amir's mystery and sin. And after that the results of it won't let them put the book away. However, as Johnson (2012) notes, it ought to be understood that Amir himself is not the maker of each one of those activities, he is purported-stuck principle character, who is dragged through the tale of the novel by alternate characters. Presently Amir's character will be talked about together with the impacts that made him a stuck character.

Amir's life is foreordained by some significant components. But that he is naturally introduced to an exceptionally respectable and rich family and he finds himself able to appreciate all the benefit associated with his father's status, alternate components are somewhat negative. He is certainly affected by the unlucky deficiency of his father, who passed away amid the labor, and by the feeling of blame his father feels towards his other child, whom he can't honestly acknowledge. Albeit these viewpoints are not known for the readers, they are entering Amir's life and deciding all his activities and different occasions in the book.

The unspeakability of Amir's trauma is so intense that despite having almost everything including Baba's love, he still feels a strange emptiness inside him. He is so overwhelmed by the sense of guilt that he cannot rejoice the moment of happiness, as he says:

It shouldn't have felt this way. Baba and I were finally friends. We'd gone to the zoo a few days before, seen Marjan the Lion, and I had hurled a pebble at the bear when no one was watching. We'd gone to father Khoda's Kabob House afterward...had lamb kabob with fleshy backed naan...Baba told me the stories of his travels to India and Russia...that should have been fun, spending a day like that with Baba, hearing his stories, I finally had what I'd wanted all those years. Except now that it, I felt as empty as this unkempt pool I was dangling my legs into. (Hosseini 85)

This sense of guilt and the inability to have LaCapra's (2001) work through capability, the trauma makes him feel himself as responsible for the bad luck of Hassan. He is not able to work through the moment of trauma and keeps on acting it out as he asserts, "There was a monster in the lake. It had grabbed Hassan by the ankles, dragged him to the murky bottom. I was that monster. That was the night I became an insomniac" (Hosseini 86).

About the initial fifty pages of the book are spent on telling the account of pure youth, which is irritated occasionally by the depictions of Amir's harried association with Baba, critical by the absence of Baba's adoration. There is probably every child who needs love from their guardians, if one of them is not living, the other ought to assume role of the deceased to make up for the absence. Yet shockingly for him, he appears to have a mysterious powerlessness to procure the adoration for his magnanimously liberal however candidly withholding father. Along these lines, Amir has two obstructed deterrents which hold him stuck: his yearning for a mother and his father's adoration.

This longing to have a mother has appeared differently in relation to Hassan, whose mother is alive but she has left him since he was an infant. Hassan never talks about her and Amir doesn't have enough bravery to ask him. Thus, he can't impart his agony even to the closest individual he has on the planet. He can just consider it as he envisions:"I generally thought about whether he [Hassan] imagined about her, about what she looked like, where she was. I thought about whether he ached to meet her. Did he hurt for her, the way I throbbed for my mom I had never met?" (Hosseini 6).

Amir fanatically aches for knowing something about his father. This longing for having knowledge about and discussions on his mother is partly fulfilled. From this man Amir discovers that "she had preferred almond cake with nectar and hot tea, that she we'd once utilized the expressions significantly, that she'd worried about her happiness" (Hosseini 219). In spite of the fact that, it is very little, it is a valuable memory for Amir and it is significantly more data than he has ever got from his father. As Amir reflects that Baba had constantly portrayed his mother to him in expensive strokes, in the same way as:"she was an incredible woman (...) Baba took his memories of her to the grave with him. Perhaps taking her name would have helped him to remember his blame of what he had done as such not long after she had kicked the bucket. Then again perhaps his misfortune had been so extraordinary, his torment so profound, he couldn't stand to discuss her.

The reality, that his mother has never been discussed by his father, is only one more variable adding to their poor relationship. Amir accepts his father accusing him for his mother's demise and can't overlook him for it (Hosseini 49). As though it would not be sufficient for a young man to see himself as a reason for his mother's demise, Amir likewise understands he doesn't satisfy his father's desires. This thought is affirmed when he catches the discussion of Baba and his closest companion Rahim Khan finishing with taking after words purported by his father: "If I [Baba] hadn't seen the specialist haul him out of my wife with my own particular eyes, I'd never accept he is my son" (Hosseini 20). At the point when considering Amir's future missteps, these words ought to be taken at the top of the priority list, as they are extremely solid and ready to do a ton of damage in a kid's spirit.

Taking a gander at all these viewpoints, what at the first look may have appeared to be a pure adolescence, is, as Flanagan (2012) states it, shadowed by a dim cloud; a disturbed association with his [Amir] inaccessible father. While perusing a percentage of the first pages, the readers effectively see the amount Amir experiences the absence of affirmation and enthusiasm from his father. He finds himself able to understand that more often than not Baba goes through his activities without appreciating them. Furthermore, he can likewise feel his father's failure with him after the vast majority of these events. The flashbacks of the past keep on haunting him as he recalls: "I cried the distance back home. I recall how Baba's hand grasped around the driving wheel. Gripped and unclenched. Basically, I will always remember Baba's valiant endeavors to disguise the sickened look all over as we drove in quiet" (Hosseini 19).

This absence of distinguishing from his father does not result in that Amir would not love his father. Very opposite, he cherishes him all that much and is glad to be his child: "He [Baba] motioned to me [Amir] to hold his cap for him and I was happy to, on the grounds that then everybody would see that he was my father, my Baba" (Hosseini 13). it can be said that what Amir craves for most in life is the warmth from his father that he questions he will ever know (Johnson, 6). Furthermore the best way to get this love and distinguishing is to fulfill the dream of his father.

After some disillusioning endeavors, for example, a soccer or Buzkashi competition, Baba has rolled out to improvement his child into a man, he proposes: "I think perhaps you win the [kite flying] competition this year" (Hosseini 49). It is a defining moment for Amir. As Baker (2003) notes, winning a yearly kite-flying challenge, where young man fight for pride outfitted with kite strings covered in ground glass, may be truly Amir's last opportunity to pick up his father's adoration. Amir has a trust now. He is a decent kite contender and just in the event that he won. It would change a ton. Amir makes a determination:

I was going to win. There was no other practical interview. I was going to win, and I was going to run that last kite. At that point I'd bring it home and demonstrate to it to Baba. Reveal to him for the last time that his child was commendable. At that point perhaps my life as an apparition in this house would at long last be over. I let myself dream: I envisioned discussion and giggling over supper... (Hosseini 49)

Also truly, after an exceptionally exciting portrayal of the kite battles, Amir with the backing of Hassan wins the competition. While Hassan, who is the best kite runner in entire Kabul, begins his approach to discover their rival's kite whose string he and Amir have cut, Amir envisions the scene when he and Hassan will as one bring the kite they have cut and found.

The aforementioned portrayal of everyday life in Kabul has been set forth by Hosseini, the novelist, in a masterly manner. The inclusion of kite flying, the love between a son and a father, the pinching absence of a mother in the life of a child, and the friendship between two children have been presented as events of everyday life from people who are full-fledged human being, thus setting the stage for something unusual to take place. Later on, the novelist, foregrounds the extraordinary trauma of war in the lives of these people and goes on to let the readers feel the difference between the two extremes of peaceful life in the streets of Kabul and the post-war scenario where these people yearn for their country which they have left due to the curse of the war.

After discussing the whole lot goodness hovering around Amir's life, Hosseini then turns towards portraying the opposite, that is the ravages of war and it impact on Amir's happy life. As expressions such as 'happily ever after' are uncommon outside the universe of tall tales, Amir wins the competition, yet loses something considerably more essential. Hayes (2007) calls it the loss of innocence, and burden to carry throughout his life. She says that: "he [Amir] was simply starting to consider some main problems in life, when the steadfast day of both triumph and thrashing changed his life until the end of time. Growing was no more progressive. He had all of a sudden been pushed into adulthood (Hayes, 2007, p.12).

Amir loses his guiltlessness and finds himself underhanded. Tragically, he not just finds that there is shrewdness in his general surroundings (here displayed by Assef who assaults Hassan) additionally within him, when he abstains from helping Hassan. Presently, the distinguishing of his father doesn't appear to be so vital. Amir frantically needs to admit himself, to pick up reclamation; however, again, he has not overcome and sufficiently solid to face the potential outcomes. So, he stays in hush. This is the unspeakability of trauma, which has been discussed at the start of this chapter. Amir has been hit by the trauma of being unfaithful to his friend but he cannot speak about it, while he will, at the same time be haunted by the memories of that traumatizing scene. Amir says: "I opened my mouth, almost said something. Almost the rest of my life might have turned out differently if I had. But I didn't. I just watched Paralyzed" (Hosseini 73).

Amir feels responsible for what happened to Hassan. "School gave me an excuse to say in my room for long hours. And, for a while, it took my mind off what had happened that winter, what I had let happen" (Hosseini 91). The more Amir avoids reconnecting to everyday life, the more he will have problems in coping with and overcoming the trauma, as Herman (1992) suggests that the third stage in a traumatized person's recovery is to reconnect to everyday life.

Moreover, as a survivor of trauma feels guilty for having survived the incident and blames him or herself for the mishap, Amir lashes out at himself in anger: "I hurled the pomegranate at him. It stuck him in the chest, exploded in a spray of red pulp... Hit me back!' I snapped... I wished he would. I wished he'd give me the punishment I craved, so maybe I'd finally sleep at night" (Hosseini 92). This is typical of the survivors of trauma that they consider themselves responsible for the trauma.

The association with Baba begins to chill off once more. Also as from wickedness normally emerges nothing else than fiendishness, Amir, who can't stand being close to Hassan, shrouds some cash and his wrist watch in Hassan's room and cases that Hassan took the cash as an approach to dispose of him. Amir is stuck once more; it is not a need of his father's adoration yet his wrongdoing and regret which impact his life starting now and into the foreseeable future don't permit him to be free.

In the wake of moving to America, Amir's circumstances show signs of improvement and recovery from the trauma. He is currently ready to remain for what he needs. He doesn't study pharmaceutical as his father wishes; however, he now deals with turning into an expert author and weds Soraya, a lady he adores, despite the fact that she is joined by an awful notoriety. Presumably, it may be the way that he knows she also committed errors throughout her life yet had the capacity to overcome them that makes him adore her significantly more. Together, they deal with Baba until he kicks the bucket of growth.

At last, both Amir and Baba have got the capacity to figure out how to one another. Baba reads Amir's stories and regards him. Thus, both Baba and Amir make a concerted effort to adapt according to new situation, work through the hard time to deal with the realities of life and reconnect to life. Both the characters, amid all the haunting of the past, try to work through this situation in a bid not to be overwhelmed by the severity of the circumstances in their country. It can be said that aside from their incapacity of having an infant, his existence with Soraya is cheerful.

However, Amir infrequently recollects Hassan and thinks about how, if whatsoever, he lives in Afghanistan and soon, he is going to find him. One day, Rahim Khan calls from Pakistan and asks Amir to come and be good once again. This is an appeal Amir is not ready to deny. Nonetheless, in the wake of landing in Pakistan and finding out about Rahim Khan's and Hassan's life in Kabul, about Hassan's child Sohrab, about Hassan and his wife being dead and in particular about Hassan being his illegitimate sibling, Rahim Khan uncovers the genuine motivation behind why he has asked Amir to come. The reason is to discover Sohrab in a Kabul shelter and bring him back. This is the time when Amir has once again a decision to make for himself. He can either venture back from a shadowed rear way as he did it on that winter night, or he can emerge for himself and reimburse the obligation he has made. He picks the second alternative.

By coming to Pakistan, Amir has been hauled out from his wellbeing and solace yet he takes the tenet over his life and holds it with a determination and fearlessness so ordinary for his father. There is no other choice for him than to return with Sohrab. Despite the fact that towards the end of the novel, he demonstrates the absence of understanding for the youngster's spirit tormented by the passing of his guardians, life in the orphanage and ill-use by Aseef, who made a profession as a Talib officer, and adds to Sohrab's suicide endeavor, he completes his trip effectively. He finishes a bizarre circle of occasions. Hayes sees his voyages as one illustration of the way of round time in *The Kite Runner*. In many ways, life continues rehashing itself: the parallel existences of Ali and Baba, Hassan and Amir and even Aseef and Amir. Life holds returning on itself in loads of ways (Hosseini 9). At the point when Amir come back home with little Sohrab and runs a kite only for an indication of grin all over, this round of time closes. Furthermore after all it appears to end cheerfully.

At the point when Amir comes back to Pakistan to visit the feeble Rahim Khan, he learns of Hassan's child, Sohrab. Indeed, even in a blurry picture, Amir sees the similarity to the partner of his youth. Following Rahim Khan's suggestion to Amir to rescue Sohrab, Amir, at first, rejects the thought, for the undeniable dangers it involves. In a matter of seconds, however, his sense of guilt rouses him to endeavor the salvage, with the supposition that another person will tend to the kid once they come back to Pakistan.

In order to give a background to how Amir dealt with Hassan in his childhood, it is apt to say that Amir, right from the start, has been pitiless to Hassan, the same degree as he values his fellowship and adores him in his own way. In any case why is it so? Hassan is adored by Baba and their companionship is backed by him too, so where is the issue? The principal weak link in their relationship can be seen in the way that Amir is a Pashtun and Hassan a Hazara. These two ethnic gatherings are very opposing and Hazara viewed as a lower race have experienced, compared to the Pashtuns. "Ali and Baba were likewise near to one another and spent their adolescence together. On the other hand, as

Amir notices, Baba never alludes to Ali as his companion" (Hosseini 22). What's more, Amir doesn't think himself as Hassan's companion. As Hosseini says:

Don't bother that we taught one another to ride a bike with no hands, or to manufacture a completely utilitarian custom made of a cardboard box. Don't worry about it that we spent whole winters flying kites, running kites. (...) Never mind any of those things. Since history isn't anything but difficult to succeed, nor is religion. At last, I was a Pashtun and he was a Hazara, I was Sunni and he was Shia and nothing was steadily going to change that. Nothing. (Hosseini 22)

Also without a doubt, it is not simple to beat all these angles. However, the more vital thing deciding their relationship may be Amir's envy. It is Hassan who dependably stands before him and battles for him if needed. Amir acknowledges the amount of his father wishes to be able to emerge for himself and the amount Hassan is in his valor like his father. This may be the purpose behind Amir's repulsive jokes or looking down at Hassan for his lack of education. All things considered, books appear to be the main territory where Amir is superior to Hassan. Yet even here, Hassan demonstrates his ethical predominance. At the point when Amir plays a trap on him and rather than standard perusing from the book, he makes up his own particular story, Hassan is awed and admires it as: "The best story, you've read me in a long time" (Hosseini 26).

Now and then, it is significantly harder to excuse an ideal than a bad habit. Also it unquestionably is here for Amir. What's more, it deteriorates, when Amir sells out Hassan. In spite of the fact that Hassan is the person who has been harmed, he stays steadfast and makes the life for

Amir deplorable. At last, this steadfastness determines in Amir's fruitful endeavor to pursue Hassan away.

All things considered, measuring all the terrible attributes of Amir and his heaping one oversight one another, it can be expressed that: "Amir is a profoundly defective young man, failing to possess the mettle which his father has so inexhaustibly, yet I likewise felt him to be exceptionally amiable and sympathetic" (Bond 89). The readers can't simply judge him, they are compelled to feel with him: " Amir's double c-crossing of Hassan is trustworthy and reasonable in human terms, aside from society, and his long haul regret is not astounding" (Whipple 77). Also, the readers are not just compelled to feel Amir's feelings, they are likewise dragged into the minute, the same as him, they are impacted by same perspectives as Amir and they must be humane as they are liable to the same as he may be.

Amir feels like he is a bad person. "I wanted to tell them all that I was the snake in the grass, the monster in the lake. I wasn't worthy of this sacrifice; I was a liar, a cheat, and a thief" (Hosseini 105).

Even in adulthood, Amir cannot get away from these feelings. "There was so much goodness in my life. So much happiness, Wondered whether I deserved any of it" (Hosseini 183). "Perhaps something, someone, somewhere, had decided to deny me fatherhood for the things I had done. Maybe this was my punishment, and perhaps justly so." (Hosseini 188).

Hosseini has an amazing capacity to detain the reader in horrific, shatteringly prompt scenes, at least, in the episode in which Hassan is degraded. The outcome is a sickening impression of complicity. Like Amir, the reader watches the anguish and does nothing. (...) True insidiousness, he recommends, comes when great individuals permit such horrific incidents to take place. Readers feel the pinch of the incident which has been foregrounded by Hosseini in a skillful manner after showing the fun-filled activities of kite running in Kabul.

In spite of the fact that Hassan's life is taken care of just in the first part of the book and afterward it is simply left to Rahim Khan to retell whatever remains of Hassan's story are. It can be said that he is the most vital character in the novel. He is the pivotal point in the entire novel rotates around. Accordingly, his character ought to be in any event quickly covered here.

Before the real analyzing the trauma of Hassan's son, names Sohrab, it ought to be comprehended what it meant to be a Hazara in the seventies in Afghanistan. Johnson 920120 clarifies that in America, the status of Hassan and his father would be practically identical to being dark and Native American in the profound South in the 1920's in addition, Hassan is a motherless youngster. His mother left him not long after he was conceived. Once more, this is far more atrocious when a wife leaves spouse with an alternate man, she hurts her family's honor more than anything else in the Afghan society. In any case, Hassan is not a terrible youngster, influenced contrarily by all these certainties. He doesn't appear to be a miserable individual. What's more it can be asked, for what good reason it is so.

Hassan's most huge peculiarity is his capacity to discover a falling kite without really taking a gander at the sky. He doesn't have to look at the kite coming down from the sky because he knows the art of kite running more than any of his competitors. Also he carries on with his life in the same way. He knows how to carry on with a genuine living, "as he has basically acknowledged the part he's been given in life (Whipple, 2003) and he does all the better he can do with all the methods he has got. He puts his absolute entirety in all that he does and is unimaginably steadfast and truthful. He generally comes clean and he thinks others do too" (Hosseini 48).

The faithfulness is most evident in his relationship towards Amir and it even now and then makes Hassan lie. Hassan dependably takes the fault for what Amir did when some devilishness was discovered out (Johnson, 2012). Furthermore, he does this even when he will be unreasonably faulted of taking. He claims to be liable and ensures Amir's safety:

This was Hassan's last relinquish for me. On the off chance that he'd said no, Baba would trust him on the grounds that we all knew Hassan never lied. Furthermore if Baba trusted him, then I'd be charged; I would need to clarify and I would be uncovered for what I truly was. Baba would never, ever excuse me. (Hosseini 91)

Also that prompts an alternate comprehension: "Hassan knew. He knew I'd seen him in that back road, that I'd remained there and done nothing" (Hosseini 91). This dependability and acknowledgement of his part in life has its launching presumably in Hassan's and Ali's religion and their solid faith in God and his will. The way that Hassan acknowledges his part does not imply that he doesn't long anything. It ought to be said that he wishes not to be uneducated and when he turns into a father, pretty much as all the folks, he wishes the best for his kid.

As he says in his letter to Amir: "I dream that my child will grow up to be a decent individual, a free individual and a vital person" (Hosseini 191). A decent, free and imperative individual, nonetheless as Hassan seemed to be, as the opportunity and capacity does not originate from the outside world however from within every person. Furthermore, as Lencz (2003) focuses that, there is substantially more sense and significance in carrying on with a genuine soul and heart than in being an apparently essential government official choosing about the lives of millions of individual without truly understanding the life.

While in Kabul, Amir is stunned to discover that Aseef purchased the young man from an overfull shelter. At the point when Amir requests the young man's discharge, Aseef demands the battle until the very end. With minimal decision for another alternative, Amir experiences a ruthless beating on account of Aseef. At last, Sohrab shoots Aseef with his slingshot, thus rescuing Amir. Sohrab and Amir escape the house in the midst of Aseef's horrifying yells.

When they come back to Pakistan and Amir leaves the clinic, they discover that the guaranteed guardians never existed. Amir chooses to watch over Sohrab himself and offers to take the kid back to America. Sohrab shows reluctance and asks that he never needed to come back to a shelter. Then again, the legal counsel in Pakistan prompts for an impermanent spell in a Pakistani shelter that Amir could go back to the United States and organize the kid's adoption. Sohrab, overpowered by such a prospect, endeavors to commit suicide. Notwithstanding Amir's urgent requests and conciliatory sentiment, the kid stays stoic for a considerable length of time.

Being unable to work through the trauma, as according to LaCapra (2001) working through the trauma enables a victim to take the incident as part of his various life events and makes the recovery from trauma a bit easier, Sohrab, on most occasions, seems lost in his thoughts or may be haunted by whatever he witnessed. While leaving,

Farid stops at the doorway of the hotel room, says good bye to Sohrab and then expects him to respond. However, Sohrab remains indifferent to everything as he "Just rocked back and forth, his face lit by the silver glow of the images flickering across the screen" (Hosseini 312). Following what Herman suggests as the third stage for the survivors of trauma in the form of reconnection to life, this description proves that Sohrab has not been recovering from the trauma as he is unable to reconnect to life.

Following Caruth's (1992) remarks that the survivor of an incident of trauma experiences the flashbacks of the incident concerned, Sohrab is also haunted by events from his past life. As soon as he, while standing with Amir, sees a, "horse drawn cart clip-clopped by in the parking lot and little bells dangled from the horse's neck and jingled with each step," he starts thinking about the time when he was sexually abused. He feels the guilt. This reminds Sohrab of being sexually abused by the Taliban as he, "starts crying, softly, silently." This also leads Sohrab to ask, "Will God put me in hell for what I did to that man" (Hosseini 318). Sohrab's reaction does that he blames himself for what the Taliban did to him. This is another symptom of PTSD.

Sohrab shows more signs of self-blame when he asks, "Do you think father is disappointed in me ?" The thought of Sohrab's parents and friends not seeing him right now makes him cry when he, "wipes his face with the sleeve of his shirt. It burst a bubble of spittle that had formed on his lips. He buries his face in his hands and wept a long time." He goes on to blame himself by saying, "But sometimes I'm glad they're mot here anymore. Because I don't want them to see me...I'm so dirty and full of sin (p. 319). As Erickson outlines that the survivors of trauma will hardly trust their fellow beings, Sohrab also has trouble trusting other people by saying " what if you get tired of me? What if your wife doesn't like me? I don't want to go to other orphanage, he said. His pillows were soaking the pillow" (Hosseini 327). In fact, Sohrab wants the people around him again, especially Amir, to make him belief that he will not leave him for the trauma to hit him again. He wants safety, which according to Herman (1992), is the first stage in a person's recovery from trauma.

Once Amir seemingly breaks his promise with Sohrab to go back to orphanage, Sohrab goes into a state of panic. The memories seem like flashbacks for Sohrab's mind because he starts pleading, "Please promise, you won't! Oh God, Amir agha! Please promise you won't! he wept into my shirt until his tears dried, until his shaking stopped and his frantic pleas dwindled to indecipherable mumbles" (Hosseini 303). This is perfectly in accordance with what Erickson (1994) recommends, saying that the survivor keeps on worrying if the same moment of trauma may return and hit him again. The memories are so bad that Sohrab falls asleep crying, Amir then remembered that this is how children deal with terror. They fall asleep.

Sohrab's fear of going back to the orphanage gave him the reason to commit suicide by cutting himself by Amir's razor. This left him, "pale with a large purple bruise in the crease of his right arm" (Hosseini 354). Here again, the trauma of the war that Sohrab has endured has been so immense that he keeps on worrying if his close ones will desert him and he will again be left for the traumatic incident. This is the reason why Erickson (1994) and Miller (2003) suggest that the reaction from the surroundings towards the victim of trauma is extremely important. As Herman (1994) says that the first stage of recovering from trauma is the sense of safety in the life of the victim, Sohrab badly needs that safety. His fears of being left behind send shivers down his spine because he doesn't want to re-experience whatever he has already witnessed.

When Sohrab is on 24-hour-suicide watch in the hospital, Amir tries to cheer him up, and tells him that he is not going to the orphanage. However, remaining true to what Erickson (1994) suggests that the victim fears that the trauma will hit him again, Sohrab is seen having problems trusting others, such as Amir, because Sohrab only, "holds [a] glance, and then looked away" when Amir is trying to cheer him up. Sohrab has a, "face that is set like stone. His eyes were still lightless, vacant, the way I had found them when I had pulled him out of the bathtub" (Hosseini 354). He has been frozen in the moment as he is neither able to use the problem-focused mechanism nor the emotion-centered strategy, as outlined by Miller (2000). Sohrab's witnessing of the ravages of war in his country and its impact on his own life have been so traumatic that he is simply unable to use any of the coping strategies; as a result, he opts for committing suicide but survives it.

Thus, Sohrab shows signs of PTSD by telling Amir that he is tired of everything, proving that he has been overwhelmed by the overall situation. Sohrab, then, brings his hand to his throat, "I want my old life back, I want Father and Mother Jan. I want Sasa. I want to olay with Rahim Khan Sahib in the garden. I want to live in our house again." (Hosseini 354). In this way, he mourns the loss of his previous life, which was full of peace around him. Herman (1994) asserts that the victim of trauma mourns the losses, and that this is the second stage of recovery from trauma. Here, Sohrab reconstructs the trauma because he is remembering whatever he witnessed in the past and, thus, mourns the losses. At this stage, according to Herman

(1994), the victim of trauma continues his journey towards his recovery from the trauma. This happens to Sohrab when he has been assured that he will be taken away from the site of the war, and he is thus sure that his safety has been established. Only then, Sohrab, mourns the losses, which are in the form of his life in the past.

However, the third stage of Herman's (1994) model, according to which the survivor of trauma should reconnect to everyday life, does not apply on Sohrab, who remains silent and ignores interaction with others. Leaving the people around him to guess how big a sorrow he has witnessed or suffered, as Amir wonders if Sohrab had, "...seen the Taliban drag his parents out into the street" (Hosseini 317). This silence, which goes on to show the unspeakability of Sohrab's trauma, shows the immense size of his trauma that then shapes his very identity. As a result, Sohrab stays aloof from the rest of the world and fails to recover from trauma.

The unspeakability of Sohrab's trauma is so huge that he, after going to America, remains silent all the time. Amir sees this as an effect from all the abuse he had undergone due to the war in his country, as he says, "It was the silence of the one who has taken cover in a dark place, curled up all the edges and tucked them under" (Hosseini 361). In order to fully recover from the trauma that he has experienced, he, according to Herman (1992), needs to reconnect to everyday life but he simply fails to do so. The burden of his witnessing that has resulted in his unpleasant memories does not allow him to reconnect to everyday life.

Amir sees Sohrab's unwillingness to communicate with others, as former says, "Sohrab walked like he was afraid to leave behind footprints. He moved as if not to stir the air around him. Mostly, he slept." (p. 365) Thus, unlike the eagerness on part of some characters to tell others about the destruction they have seen, Sohrab decides to remain silent in a bid to tell the world how unrepresentable and unspeakable his sorrows and those of his countrymen are. This unrepresentability on the part of Sohrab is due to the fact that he has formed an exclusive identity for himself which is hallmarked by the absence of structures, through which he could speak of his trauma. His silence shows that his trauma is of such exceptional nature that it, according to Caruth (1995), is being portrayed as unrepresentable, unspeakable, and that it is experienced as an absence.

The trauma of Sohrab and many other Afghans, who have gone through the tribulations of such overwhelming nature find it impossible to reconnect to life. Sohrab's condition is also significant in one other aspect: the nature of trauma that he has experienced is too big for him to understand upon occurrence, as Caruth (1995) mentions the impossibility to understand trauma upon occurrence. Since the nature of the incident is of such magnitude that it poses questions of un-speakability and un-representability, it becomes equally difficult for historians to record the incident upon occurrence, mainly because the survivors, who happen to witness it, are unable to speak their mind or relate whatever they witnessed. Thus, it is then left to writers of fiction to represent the trauma later on, because one of the hallmarks of trauma is its emphasis on delayed reaction to whatever has taken place. So, the analysis of the novels is decisive in unearthing the history that could not be recorded by historians when the incident took place.

This part of the study provides answer to the first research question: keeping in view the concepts of *Acting Out and/or Working Through* in trauma theory, how do the traumatized characters in the selected Afghan fictional narratives in English articulate their witnessing of trauma, and what measures do the traumatized characters take to cope with the overwhelming incident of war in order to recover from the trauma and reconnect to everyday life? The study discusses how different the reactions of different characters have been towards the impending nature of trauma that they witnessed in the form of the war in their country. This goes on to show how skillfully literature represents the unrepresentable nature of trauma and how vocally do fictional narratives speak of the phenomenon that is marked by its unspeakability. The aforementioned analysis shows how varying the responses of different people have been when they are impacted by the overwhelming nature of trauma. Thus, this part of the study, in conjunction with the previous chapter, answers the first question of this study.

CHAPTER FIVE

CONCLUSION

The concluding remarks of this dissertation hover back to the issues, which were brought up in the space of its opening pages identifying with trauma's characteristic spatio-fleeting structure – an unforeseen and hence overwhelming knowledge that is not seen as it happens but rather is over and over reestablished later and somewhere else as opposed to memory, accordingly offering principal difficulties to assumption of referentiality and reality, and additionally resisting customary ideas of time and space. The emergency that trauma perpetually involves raises issues of representation, memory and witnessing with particular ramifications for scholarly studies. Moreover, trauma fiction presents readers with fundamentally new issues of explication. As trauma is not completely experienced upon event and just accessible belatedly and somewhere else, it can then just be spoken to through our inability to have time and space, described through spatial (dis)locations and temporal (dis)ruptions.

An "Unclaimed experience," as Caruth (1996) calls it, trauma is a phenomenon that is not experienced upon event and, along these lines, abandons witnessing from inside the experience itself. It is this powerlessness to witness the traumatic occasion from within that, as Felman and Laub (1992) have attested, lies at the very heart of trauma. Kilby (2007) puts the point exactly: "No one has or possesses the inside view, perhaps least of all the victims, since they cannot bear witness the horror of what is happening to them" (Kilby 90).

However, nor can trauma be seen from outside. Suspended in the middle of time and space, it drifts additionally between the socio-cultural and the individual, disturbing while maintaining private/public or inside/ outside twofold refinements and fringes, which implies that it is not arranged inside or outside, but rather it converges on the limit lines in the middle of inside and outside; it is all the while a private and a public entity with both individual and socio-cultural reasons and implications. Notwithstanding the disappointment of witnessing traumatic experience from inside, then, a few difficulties to be a witness to a trauma come from the outside. Traumatic flashbacks do not develop as standard memory, which is directly narrativized, and which brings up issues as to the truthfulness of the act of witnessing. As opposed to untellable or un-communicated, the traumatic experience is not recognized from the outside as well.

As the mind of survivor of a traumatic incident records the details of the moment and s/he is usually unable to get rid of the flashbacks, the moment remains intact and is true to the core. On the one hand, the survivor suffers from the continuous remembering of the incident in the form of flashbacks of the traumatic scenes but, on the other hand, s/he works as witness to the incident. The fictional narratives,which deals with the moments of trauma, bring forth and present for public viewing the minute details of the incident, which fall a prey to the erasures of official accounts of reference, called history. These fictional narratives of trauma do not let the extraordinary details of a traumatic incident to go unnoticed or be forgotten; rather they keep on repeating themselves in their raw form just like these incidents, along with all their naked brute force, which hit the trauma affected person upon occurrence. Thus, these trauma narrative serve not only the survivors of the traumatic incicent concerned by keeping on telling the world about their world of hurt, but also remind the living of the sacrifices of the ones, who could not survive the overwhelming impact of the trauma that they witnessed.

In the same vein, the selected novel for this study portray the condition of the traumatized characters and bring forth whatever goes through their minds, thus not only bringing forth their sufferings due to the ongoing wars but, at the same time, also making sure that the statements of the traumatized characters are able to fill in any lacunae in historical accounts. Interestingly, the portrayal of characters such as Hosseini's Amir, Hassan and Sohrab as well as their development in the face of post-soviet-attack caused traumatic disorder has been so true to the traumatic theories that one is compelled to think as if Hosseini, the novelist, has been masterfully adept in this traumatic analysis with special reference to the concepts of working through, acting out, and PTSD. The writer has been able to achieve his target by creating such realistic accounts of these traumatized characters and their coping with trauma mechanism that their actions in the face of incident of war and reactions to the impending Soviet attacks have been perfectly in line with the theories dealing with trauma. Since the overwhelming nature of traumatic incident makes it difficult for historians to record the moment of trauma, and the survivors are prone to show a delayed reaction to whatever they witnessed. Such fictional narratives, which came under investigation in this study, better portray the impact of trauma long after it has taken place.

Thus, the accounts of the ravages of war as presented by these fictional characters and the coping with trauma mechanisms have been convincing and, consequently, qualify for augmenting the concerned historical accounts. Anyone, who wants to study the minutest of details of the ravages of war in any country, will be greatly benefitted if s/he consults such fictional narratives, which are written by the native writers. The study thus answers the first research question: Keeping in view LaCapra's (2001) concepts of *Acting out* and/or *Working Through* in trauma theory, how do the traumatized characters in the selected narrative in English articulate their witnessing of trauma, and what measures do the traumatized characters take to cope with the overwhelming incident of war in order to recover from the trauma and reconnect to everyday life?

As Hosseini's The Kite Runner deals with the trauma of war-hit characters and brings forth their reactions and working through strategies and in which the war-hit characters are forced to leave their country, to their neighboring countries due to the war torn conditions of the time. It brings forth the fact how these characters are continuously haunted by the memories of their country and how, while living in other countries as migrated individuals amid the whole developed infrastructure, they are continuously haunted by the memories of their country and the troubles and tribulations they have to go through as a result of the war. The writer juxtaposes the initially-portrayed peaceful life of Baba, Amir, Hassan, Ali and other characters in Kabul with their post-trauma life that is full of material facilities but completely devoid of mental peace due to the continuous flashbacks of trial and tribulations while leaving Afghanistan and after settling down in the foreign countries.

The writer, thus, fills in the gaps, if any, regarding the problems and traumas of the Afghan people during the times of war. Thus, it answers the second question: in what ways can the trauma of an individual character in the selected novel be ascribed to the collective war-impacted ravages in Afghan society?

So, the study of history, especially if that is related to an incident of trauma, can be best augmented by fictional narratives written by writers who, one way or the other, are impacted by, and are implicated in, that trauma.

Literature, as Caruth (1995) says, has the capacity to represent the details of the un-representable nature of trauma, adding that this is the specialty of literature to cater for this complicated concept, to comprehend it, and express its peculiarity of trauma. Where history becomes handicapped in taking liberty with the details of a trauma as the former as to remain to the factual truth, Literature amends for this inability of history by providing an imaginative tinge of the details of the trauma and presents what may not be factual due to the fact that the names and dates may not be truthful, but the mental processes that the survivor of trauma experiences, the reactions that s/he comes up with, the aftermath of the ravages of the incident, and the coping mechanism adopted by the survivor are as true as felt, experienced, and dealt with by the real survivors of trauma. The only difference is that the novelist uses literary imagination to mold the whole experience of trauma in order to make it suitable for the representation of this un-representable incident. So, once the truth issue of these accounts is settled, any inquiry into the history of such incidents of trauma is recommended to be augmented by such fictional narratives. In this way, the study also provides a detailed answer to the third research question: Following Cathy Caruth's footsteps, can the portrayal of trauma of the individual characters in the selected novel add something to the history which is recorded under the traditional documentary evidence?

Keeping in view of the importance of fictional narratives dealing with trauma in the study of history, and in the light of this study, it is recommended for the other researchers to use trauma literary theory to investigate other works of literature, which deals with other incidents of trauma. It is pertinent to mention here that researchers can carry out studies of fictional narratives, which deals with natural disasters as well; for example the havoc caused by floods, destruction resulting from the earthquakes, and the overwhelming impact of other disasters as portrayed in literature. Trauma analysis of literature emanating from other war-hit countries such as Iraq, Syria, and other countries, which are not in that much limelight as the technologically- advanced countries are, will be of great help in supplementing the histories of incidents of trauma in these countries.

The study also recommends for the perspective researchers to embark upon the trauma study of literature that deals with the impact of the suicide attacks on the mind of survivors of such attacks in other countries. This will provide a personalized history, which is full of the minute details of the ravages of the suicide attacks in other nations by bringing forth the torturous survival accounts of the survivors of these blasts and the sorrows of the ones, who are left behind to mourn their losses in the attacks.

The accounts will take the historical records of such deadly incidents much ahead of mere terming or naming the events as suicide attacks, a tag attached to these incidents, and come up with the complete package of how sabotaging and traumatic these incidents are for those who witness them.

There is also a scope for future researchers to carry out trauma analysis of fictional narratives, dealing with other issues which results in the losses and destruction of not only the physical properties but the loved ones from the survivors and thereafter their reaction to this overwhelming nature of incident. Moreover, instead of researching the already saturated areas like the Holocaust studies and the post 9/11 fiction, it is recommended for researchers to look for new avenues and study fictional narratives, which deal with the trauma that is caused not only by war but also by sexual violence and natural calamities, such as earthquakes and floods, which wipe out complete communities.

Keeping in view the aforementioned emphasis on looking out for new avenues for carrying out trauma analyses of fictional narratives, there is also a need to study Non-Anglophonic literature. Prospective researchers in Pakistan can study and analyze literature, concerning traumatic incidents, in Urdu and other local languages. This will not only help them looking into issues which are of indigenous nature but will also enrich the history of the region. Other researchers in other parts of the world can also carry out trauma analyses of such literature produced in their own local languages. Researchers, who are working on fiction that is produced in Pakistan, can analyse the trauma caused by the partition of the Indian subcontinent, or, for that matter, the trauma resulting from the Fall of

Dhaka in 1971. One of the examples in such cases can be to carry out a trauma analysis of Saadat Hasan Manto's Urdu narratives titled *Toba Tek Singh* and *Tandha Gosht* in order to study the trauma of people, who suffered during the partition in 1947.

This stress on indigenizing or localizing trauma scholarship is the need of the hour in order for researchers to avoid falling a prey to the politics of trauma, which revolves around the Holocaust studies, post 9/11 scholarship and trauma related to the technologically advanced countries. The overemphasis on Holocaust studies in the form of the establishment of Holocaust studies centres and the resulting scholarship through excessive publications in this field has deprived trauma studies of its earlier universalizing concept which, in the words of Caruth (1995), was established on the slogan that says that we are implicated in each other's trauma, unfortunately, the politics of trauma has made its previously non-advocacy movement into a purely European or American enterprise, which can best be balanced through carrying out analyses and details studies of trauma narratives, dealing with the developing nations.

In this case, it is pertinent to mention and emphasize here for future researchers to be cautious while using models and theories of Western scholarship for analyzing trauma related incidents and issues in their local cultural settings. There is a need to be careful in this case as the coping with trauma mechanisms as well as the overall reaction to a traumatic incident from survivor may vary from culture to culture. As the oft-criticized Eurocentric dealing and projection of trauma studies show that all the theories and models dealing with the ways in which trauma survivors cope with the incident are developed in accordance with the value and cultures of western societies, the applications of these theories and models for the analysis of non-Western fictional narratives without any adjustment thereof may not be appropriate. The reason for this unsuitability of the existing trauma models by the Western scholarship is that the values, belief system, and the overall standards of life of people living in West are different from those living in others parts of the world. Thus, the development of purely indigenous models is needed in order to cater for the local needs as this will show how differently people, living in different parts of the world, act out or work through their trauma.

Lastly, the very spirit of trauma studies, which according to Caruth (1995) is that we are implicated in each other's trauma, requires of researchers in this field to investigate the individual traumas of societies irrespective of how powerful and/or technologically advanced they are, because one person's trauma is a stimulus for the recalling of another person's trauma. Once again, when Craps (2008) critics the Eurocentric blind spots of trauma theory, asserting that trauma theory has been produced in Europe and United States in 1990s, and since then, it has been discussing traumas like the Holocaust, and then later on, 9/11, he calls for research on the traumas of nations which are not as powerful as compared to other nations. As Craps (2008) argues that "trauma with equal, if not greater regularity" has been seen and experienced elsewhere (Caruth 9), he draws the attention of researchers to divert it from the highly saturated field of studying the trauma of advanced nations to the trauma that has been taking place to so many other people in several other places. If that is done, and if the very inclusive nature of trauma studies is maintained with its true spirit, the resulting analyses of fictional narratives dealing with trauma will greatly dissect the very history of any society concerned, and will thus enrich the very record, called history, irrespective of whose trauma it is and where has it taken place. What is being enriched and made more realistic through these analyses of fictional narratives of trauma is not an individual or a nation, but history.

Bibliography

Aexander C, Jeffery. *"Cultural Trauma and Collective Identity"* Berkeley: University of California Press, 2004.

Caruth, Cathy. *Unclaimed Experience: Trauma, Narrative, and History.* Baltimore: John Hopkins University Press, 1996.

Caruth, Cathy. *Trauma: Exploration in Memory.* Baltimore: John Hopkins University Press, 1995.

Freud, Sigmund. *"Beyond the Pleasure Principle"* Translated by James Strachey. Norton Press, 1961.

Freud, Sigmund. "Moses and Monotheism" London: The Hogarth Press, 1939.

Felman, Shoshanna. *Testimony: Crises of Witnessing In Literature, Psychoanalysis and History.* New York: Routledge P, 1992.

Hosseini, Khalid. *The Kite Runner.* London: Bloomsbury, 2004.

Herman, Judith. Trauma and Recovery: From Domestic Abuse to Political Terror. London: Basic Books, 1992. .

Kolk, Vander. Psychological Trauma. Boulevard: American Psychiatric Association, 1987.

Laub, Dory. *Testimony: Crises of Witnessing in Literature, Psychoanalysis and History.* New York: Routledge P, 1992.

Laplanche, Jean. The Language of Psychoanalysis. Translated by Donald Nicholson. New York: Norton Press, 1974.

Tal, Kali. World of Hurts: Reading the literature of Trauma. Cambridge: Cambridge University Press, 1996.

LaCapra, Dominick. *Writing History, Writing Trauma*. Baltimore: John Hopkins University Press, 2001.

LaCapra, Dominick. *Representing the Holocaust: History, Theory Trauma*. Ithaca: Cornell University Press, 1994.

Whitehead, Anne. *Trauma Fiction*. Edinburgh: Edinburgh University Press, 2004.

www.ingramcontent.com/pod-product-compliance
Lightning Source LLC
Chambersburg PA
CBHW031358160726
47993CB00003B/1023